WRITE
OUT
LOUD

Use the **Story To College** Method,
Write Great Application Essays,
and Get into Your Top Choice College

CAROL BARASH, PhD

Mc
Graw
Hill
Education

New York Chicago San Francisco Athens London Madrid
Mexico City Milan New Delhi Singapore Sydney Toronto

3 4 5 6 7 8 9 10 11 12 13 14 15 16   QVS/QVS   19 18 17 16 15

ISBN   978-0-07-182828-4
MHID   0-07-182828-1

e-ISBN 978-0-07-182829-1
e-MHID   0-07-182829-X

Library of Congress Cataloging-in-Publication Data

Barash, Carol.
   Write Out Loud : 12 tools for telling your story and getting into a great college / Carol Barash, PhD.
      pages cm
   Includes bibliographical references.
   ISBN 0-07-182828-1
  1. College applications. 2. Essay—Authorship. 3. Storytelling. I. Title.
II. Title: Twelve tools for telling your story and getting into a great college.
   LB2351.5.B37 2014
   378.1'616—dc23

                                                          2013026953

Story To College and Moments Method are registered trademarks of Story To College and may not be used without the author's written permission.

Interior design by THINK Book Works

Credits

Page 49: Chapter-opening quote from *Men in Dark Times* by Hannah Arendt. Published by Houghton Mifflin Harcourt. Copyright by Houghton Mifflin Harcourt. Used with permission.

Page 117: Chapter-opening quote from *Wisdom for the Soul: Five Millennia of Prescriptions for Spiritual Healing*, edited by Larry Chang. Published by Gnosophia Publishers. Used with permission.

Page 137: Chapter-opening quote from *The Selected Works of T. S. Spivet* by Reif Larsen, copyright © 2009 by Reif Larsen. Used by permission of The Penguin Press, a division of Penguin Group (USA) Inc.

To Jed

CONTENTS

Foreword   ix

Carol's Story   xi

Acknowledgments   xiii

Introduction to the 12 Tools   xv

A Note to Parents   xxv

PART 1 | **Find**

CHAPTER 1 **Refresh**   3

CHAPTER 2 **Build a Bridge**   19

CHAPTER 3 **Transform Scripts to Stories**   49

CHAPTER 4 **Choose a Moment**   69

PART 2 | **Shape**

CHAPTER 5 **Tell It Out Loud**   87

CHAPTER 6 **Write It Out**   103

CHAPTER 7 **Focus Out**   117

CHAPTER 8 **Map It**   137

PART 3 # Perform

CHAPTER 9 **Magnet and Glow** 157

CHAPTER 10 **Explore Perspectives** 175

CHAPTER 11 **Raise the Stakes** 203

CHAPTER 12 **Write Out Loud** 221

PART 4 # More Tools for Your Journey

CHAPTER 13 **Sound Smarter: How to Find and Fix 10 Common Grammar Glitches** 231

CHAPTER 14 **Preparing for Interviews** 233

CHAPTER 15 **Frequently Asked Questions** 235

A Guide to the New 2013–2014 Common Application (CA4) 239

Free Resources for Students and Parents 253

Notes 255

FOREWORD

In 1997, at the age of 25, I started the SEED Foundation with my business partner, Eric Adler, whom I quickly came to admire for his masterful storytelling. The day I met Eric, he shared a story that sticks with me to this day.

Eric had been a high school physics teacher at a private college-prep school. While nearly every child who attended was from an affluent neighborhood, there was one student in his class from a low-income community who was attending on scholarship. Eric saw what this student had to go through each day just to get a good education. For example, while the rest of the students got to school thanks to a 15-minute ride from Mom or Dad, this student had to take two different buses, resulting in a commute of more than one and a half hours. The differences only began there. It was after seeing the hurdles that this student needed to overcome that Eric came up with the idea (around the same time that I did) of starting a public boarding school for students like this boy.

It wasn't just that Eric realized a student like this would benefit from a school like SEED and told me so. It was the *way* he told me. He could have told me in a few short and general sentences, but he captivated me with details of the student's life and struggles. Plus, he did it all with emotion. He emphasized words and lingered on parts of the story he thought were important.

Eric continued to tell this story. He told it to everyone with the same conviction as he had told it to me. He told it to legislators who were responsible for changing laws that would allow us to open our schools. He told it to potential donors we depended on to fund our schools. He shaped the story based on the listener he was trying to reach, but at its core it was the same compelling story about a boy, the struggles he fought to overcome, and how a place like SEED could make the difference.

I learned quickly from Eric and started telling stories of my own. At this point, I was completely out of my comfort zone. I was a scientist, not a storyteller. However, I had no choice; we had a school to open, and the most powerful way to spread our message was through stories. So, I told people my personal story.

I told people that our family immigrated to the United States. Both my parents believed very strongly that education was the great equalizer. With an education, you could be who you wanted to be and do what you wanted to do. My family was not wealthy. In fact, my grandfather saved every rupee he earned for his children's college education. In addition to my family's story, I told people of my belief that every child should have access to a quality education regardless of his or her background, socioeconomic status, or race.

Together, through our stories, Eric and I began to convince legislators, potential donors, and future employees to support our mission. They were inspired by our vision, they believed in our mission, and they saw that financially we had a sustainable operating model. Legislators changed laws to allow for public boarding schools in Washington, DC, donors contributed funds to build the school, and people started applying to join our team. One year later, together we opened the nation's first urban public boarding school.

By this point, I had learned to tell my story well and with conviction. By the time I met Carol Barash in 2008 (on Princeton's Annual Giving Committee), the story had expanded. It was no longer the story of two young guys trying to start a public boarding school. It was now a story about challenging society to think more broadly and more hopefully about the way that we educate our children. SEED was sending students from some of the most challenging areas of our nation's capital to the best colleges in the country. With each graduate success story, the SEED School model was challenging society to move from a conversation of "Can we do it?" to "We know we *can* do it, but are we willing to invest so that we can do it more often?" I remember Carol telling me how inspiring this model was. My 11 years of storytelling was working! In fact, at this time, Eric and I were in the midst of opening a second school in Maryland, so others must have shared Carol's opinion.

I'm still learning how to tell my stories better and more effectively, and I'm excited by how this book can help me do that. The lessons in this book have staying power. Not only will the book help you craft your essays for your top choice college, but it will also give you a toolkit to tell stories effectively for the rest of your life.

As I said, I am not a storyteller. I remember my college essay writing process. I wrote draft after draft about things I thought I *should* be telling college admissions officers, not what I wanted to tell them. While I always thought I was a good verbal communicator, I never could get the same passion down on paper. Carol breaks the storytelling craft into bite-sized pieces that make telling your story easy. While reading her book, I found myself thinking of how I was going to apply the Moments Methods to my own work at SEED today.

Today, I tell different stories than the ones I did in 1997 when Eric and I started SEED. My early stories were all about my belief in our vision and the idea of creating an education model for under-represented students. Now I can tell stories about the tangible successes of these students, many of whom are college graduates. I can tell stories about families SEED has changed, communities we've bettered, and assumptions we have challenged. These anecdotes are powerful, and with Carol's book, I'm learning to tell them better. My ultimate aim is to weave these anecdotes and successes together into a story that pushes all of us to think more boldly about what kids—all kids—can achieve and that reminds us that we have the ability and responsibility to help bring about that change.

Consider your first college essay submission to be the first story in a series of stories that you will tell for the rest of your life. Your stories will change, and you'll find new stories throughout your life. But start here, and never stop shaping and sharing stories.

—RAJIV VINNAKOTA
Co-founder and managing director
The SEED Foundation

The philosophy behind *Write Out Loud* comes from something my father said to me before he died:

> Tell the stories you can tell.
> Tell the stories only you can tell.
> Tell them as only you can tell them.

This book teaches you how to do that. Step-by-step, you will learn a process to:

> **Find** what really matters to you based on what you have already done
> **Shape** powerful connections between your own experience and what you will contribute to college and work communities
> **Perform**, making your unique vision and voice palpable not only in your application essays and interviews but in all of your spoken and written communication

It seems simple, right? Figure out what really matters to you, where you are going in college and life, and tell it to colleges honestly, based on how your own life experience fits with what those colleges offer. But it's not easy. Most high school students struggle to write college application essays they feel good about, essays that convey confidently who they are today and who they want to be in the future. Students arrive at Story To College courses trying to write the essays they think they are supposed to write—either because the topic is what their parents or teachers recommend or because they think it's what a certain college is "looking for."

How Did It Get to This Point?

I started working with high school students on college admissions essays in 1981, and through the years as I worked with students, I developed three firm rules:

1. Parents promised not to read the essays until their children were ready to show their essays to their parents.
2. If the family had another consultant reviewing the essays, I would not get involved.
3. I never touched the students' essays, not even to fix the punctuation.

I explained what needed work and I asked questions that pushed the students to explore what was most important to them, but I never did the work for students. Since I did not charge to work with students on their essays, I was able to take the high road and stick to my own rules.

When the application essay process came home to my own kitchen table when my son Zach applied Early Decision to Princeton in the fall of 2006, I saw how hard the process could be for parents as well as students. I added a couple new rules with Zach, which I suggest you show to your parents. As each of my kids reached the tortuous age of college applications, I promised them:

1. I would only read their essays when they asked me to.
2. I would ask questions but not write anything on their essays. ("That would make it feel like a school assignment," Zach said.)
3. And I would not *change* anything.

It was not easy to keep my promises! In late October 2006, very close to the Early Decision deadline, I knew Zach was working on his essay but he had not shown it to me in more than a week. On a Tuesday, after he drove to school and before I went to work, he called to ask me to bring him a history paper he had left on his desk at home. Looking for his paper, I saw a draft of the essay he was writing; it was about my father, the grandfather that he never met. I read it quickly, almost furtively, and then grabbed my keys and brief-case and ran out to deliver his paper to him at school. As I drove, I wiped tears away from my cheeks. I was touched by his honesty and his idiosyncratic syntax; with equal force, before I even realized it, I was making a mental list of ways to improve *his* essay. Because I couldn't tell him what I'd done (I had promised not to read it), I pumped all my energy into teaching him how to make the essay even more his own. These discussions crystallized the work I had done for dozens of students over the years into a framework that was replicable—and parent-proof. In many ways, those discussions were the origin of *Write Out Loud*.

Two years later, Zach was a sophomore at Princeton when he gave me the idea for this book and for my company Story To College. Before Zach left for a summer running the sports program at Worldwide Orphans Foundation (WWO) Camp Addis in Ethiopia and before his younger sister Eliana, a high school sophomore, started her summer acting course, I signed them up for an all-day storytelling workshop in New York. It made an impression on him, and later that night over pizza, he told me, "I don't think you see what's right in front of you, Mom."

I had been at somewhat of a crossroads in my career, and while I was taking a break from academia, I had been working on a memoir about my father, and studying storytelling from master storyteller Murray Nossel—the same person from whom Zach had taken his class that day. He looked up from his pizza, wiped his mouth, and said, "If you combine storytelling and the work you do every year on college essays you could help students advocate for themselves in the college admissions process and all of life." He gulped his water. "You could help a lot of people, Mom."

And thus, Story To College began.

ACKNOWLEDGMENTS

I went back and read the acknowledgments for *English Women's Poetry 1649–1714*,[1] a book I finished right before my youngest daughter was born when I was an Assistant Professor at Rutgers University.

I left Rutgers and college teaching and spent a decade gathering knowledge in the fields of humanities, computing, marketing, and development, where my spirit awakened to the joys of business. On that journey there were many different sorts of mentors, and I thank you all: Mimi Barash Coppersmith, Nan Barash, Marianne Booufall-Tynan, Jim Clifford, Christopher G. Fox, Bruce Freeman, Josh Glantz, Dan Grabon, Susan Hockey, Lisa Jordan, and Ann Kirschner.

Though I left college teaching, I never forgot the intensity of serving as a faculty advisor on the Douglass College Admissions Committee: both the way admissions readers search for students whose lives will be opened up by college, and how students' own words bring them to life in the admissions process left memories that inform *Write Out Loud*.

In fall 2008, when my daughters left home—one to Princeton and one to Andover—my world started spinning: I held on to my chair at Macaulay Honors College as light and color spun around the room, shards of broken glass flying everywhere. I knew I needed to begin something else, but I had no idea what. I owe a tremendous debt to Paul Browde and Murray Nossel, founders of Narativ, who helped me find joy in storytelling and who had the good sense to see that I needed to pursue Story To College on my own. I also want to thank Gianni Faedda and Julie Nathan, who taught me how to trust the path that was right in front of me.

Along that path I have been blessed by brilliant friends and colleagues who challenge me to create peace and prosperity for all people. More than thanks are due to Jane Aronson, Starita Boyce Ansari, Shelley Burtt, Patricia Doykos, Debby Kaminsky, Marc Williams, Alfonso Wyatt, and J'HeaLee for keeping my focus and energy in the present.

I want to thank Landmark Education for teaching me about the infinite power of language to shape reality. To my fellow travelers in the Advanced Course and Self-Expression and Leadership Program a big shout out: I promised you I would finish this book, and I kept my promise! And especially thank you to Danni Michaeli and Dave Adox, who reminded me to be "big and bold" as well as "dedicated and disciplined." Your questions and commitments sustain me again and again; this book owes its completion to all of you.

Ali McCue, Seth Weisberg, and all my friends who together are Garden State Yoga: thank you for creating and maintaining my sanctuary in the suburbs.

I am extremely grateful to Coleen O'Shea of Allen O'Shea for connecting me with the wit and wisdom of Kathy Keil at McGraw-Hill. The journey has been swift and satisfying, and I am indebted to the kindness and good sense of Susan Moore, as well as the creative spirit of Stacey Ashton, Lydia Rinaldi, Pamela Peterson, and especially Beth Schacht. Laura Lebow and Sarah Sutto have been most patient research assistants; you noticed and rescued me from many embarrassing moments.

Write Out Loud would not have been possible without the tremendously generous and talented Story To College instructors and staff who added their voices and stories to this book in many different ways: Benaifer Bhadha, Dan Blondell, Amanda D'Annucci, Michael Elka, Sammi Greene, Diana Griffin, Simone Hill, Meghan Keane, Hyeree Grace Kim, Daniel Lee, John Oros, Kyndall Parker, Rachel Stephenson, and Nicole Teitelbaum. I especially want to thank Shamayne Cumberbatch and Charles Inniss, whose spirits joined in summer 2011, generating the teaching and dialogue that became the heart of *Write Out Loud*. My thanks also to the schools and community-based organizations that have invited us to teach you and your awesome students, particularly Achievement First, Beacon School, Bronx High School of Science, Brooklyn Tech, the CollegeBound Initiative, LaGuardia Arts, Millburn High School, Millennium High School, Queens High School for the Sciences, Rutgers Preparatory School, Stuyvesant High School, Think Global School, Townsend Harris High School, University of Rochester, and the Yale-Bridgeport Partnership.

I wrote this book for the leaders of our shared future. To all of you, and especially the students who have given me permission to share the wisdom and compassion of your stories with a larger world, your stories and you have transformed me.

People who know admissions advised me on everything here that is not writing: Jeff Brenzel, Deb Heller, Patricia Redd Johnson, Joseph Latimer, Darby McHugh, Janet Rapelye, Nancy Seigel, and, especially, Steve LeMenager, who was unflinchingly honest. A special thank-you to Scott Anderson, Outreach Director for the Common Application, who answered many questions about the new Common Application. As you well know the insights about admissions belong to you; the errors and idiosyncrasies are my own.

I want to thank Carrie Greene, Shelley Krause, Joe Latimer, and Caroline Moore who read the manuscript all the way through and made many wise interventions. And Hiten Samtani, who at a critical moment asked me why I cared so much about students' stories and listened to my answer.

When I was just starting the exploration that became *Write Out Loud*, Diane Rose said, "Your father's spirit is in this book, Carol. It will be unlike anything you have written before." After a few minutes she added, "A man with a name that starts with *J* will be like a brother to you; he will help you finish." In the end there were three J-men: Jack Scotti and Jeremy Johnson, who keep this book expanding through interactive and in-school courses, and Jed, to whom this book is dedicated.

To my favorite husband, athletic inspiration, top chef, and lifelong friend, Jed Kwartler, and our devoted children, Zachary, Talia, and Eliana Kwartler, you inspire me beyond measure. Your stories and love inform everything that is best in this book—and in me. Thank you for surrounding me with such abundance.

INTRODUCTION TO THE 12 TOOLS

We do not remember days . . .
we remember moments.

—CESARE PAVESE[1]

In your college applications you take stories from your past and use them to make a credible case—a bridge—from your past to your future. *Write Out Loud* is designed to guide you—and to help you guide yourself and others—across that bridge confidently and securely. The book is organized around the questions real students ask, more than 8,000 students I have taught through more than 20 years in a variety of settings—from nationally recognized prep schools to community-based programs for students who had to leave high school for one reason or another and came back later. We all share human experiences. The stories of those experiences connect us to one another and enable us to forge community.[2]

This book is designed for you. It is not a book designed to pour in new knowledge. It is a book organized to bring out what you have and what you know. If you follow the exercises, in the order you find them here, you will build a portfolio of stories you can use not only for college application essays and interviews, but also for job and scholarship applications—any time you need to take what you have already done and make a case for others to believe in you to achieve something new in the future.

The goal of this book is to help you make the case for who you will be in college and beyond. What difference will it make to have you as a member of your college community? How can you communicate authentically with those colleges where you can make that difference best? Think of your college application as a *story about you*, a vibrant story made up of many pieces:

> Courses and grades
> Test scores
> Teachers' recommendations
> Guidance counselor's letter

> Activities and awards
> Perhaps a letter from your coach or an arts portfolio
> Sometimes an interview

Your personal essays are often the only place in the application where you get to speak in your own voice.

Students tend to talk about "the college essay," as if you only need to write one of them—sort of like a big term paper at the end of the college admissions process. Actually, if you are applying to 12 different colleges (the national average), you will probably need to write at least 13 different essays: one for each college you are applying to, plus the 650-word Personal Essay on the Common Application. Many colleges include a number of short essay questions on their supplement to the Common Application. But here's the good news: each essay is an opportunity to convey a specific aspect of your character to colleges. You can use the process you learn in *Write Out Loud* for every one of those pesky essays, and for lots of other applications too—for jobs, internships, summer programs, fellowships, and financial aid. So get ready to write a variety of essays, not just one, and since it sometimes takes some digging to find the stories that convey who you are as a person, make sure you give yourself plenty of time.[3]

After junior year—chasing down 200 extra points on the SAT or 4 more on the ACT, or pulling all-nighters to achieve that elusive 5 on an AP exam, or just keeping up your grades—you may be so exhausted that you forget why you are applying to college in the first place.[4] The essays are just another chore, another thing to check off your college to-do list. "I just want to get them done" is a refrain I hear frequently.

A New Approach

Writing successful college application essays requires a completely different approach from the grinding sprint most high school students learn to survive the demands of junior year. Personal essays flourish in a space of inquiry and discovery, a place of calm confidence and bold ambition existing side by side.[5] While teaching at Rutgers in the 1990s, I served as a faculty advisor to the Douglass College Admissions Committee, and I saw how a student's essay brought that student to life in the admissions process and often tipped the scales for one student over another. Depending on where you are applying, your essay may or may not be read in the early rounds of admission. But in situations where everything else is equal, where human beings are making a decision between students who look similar on paper, the student whose essay stands out is more likely to be admitted and considered for merit-based financial aid. The stories we tell about ourselves and other people connect us to one another and shape us into a community.

I started Story To College to explore how I might use oral storytelling to teach the widest possible range of high school and college students around the globe to advocate for themselves and what they dreamed possible, not only out loud, but especially *in writing*.[6] In order to achieve improved application essays and writing outcomes for students from all backgrounds, along with oral storytelling I researched, tested, and wove into *Write Out*

Loud innovative approaches from writing programs at selective colleges and theory and exercises from interdisciplinary performance studies.[7]

The admissions process has changed dramatically since the 1990s, when I served for two years as a faculty advisor to the admissions committee at Douglass College, Rutgers. The introduction of the Common Application in 1975 was intended to make college applications simpler for students, and the introduction of the online Common App for the class of 1999 was hailed as a move to democratize college admissions and provide everyone with equal access.[8] The exact opposite has happened. The Common App includes many questions that are confusing, even frightening for students—questions about money, race, and immigration status. The admissions and financial aid process includes dozens of different essay questions, plus a labyrinth of admission types and dates—from rolling to early action to early decision. Many of the most selective colleges have their own unique admission essays, deadlines, and requirements.[9]

In addition, the number of applicants has also increased annually as the children of baby boomers apply to college, and the number of colleges to which each student applies has edged up from 8 in 1989 to 12 in 2010.[10] To help students and parents manage this complicated and shifting application system, an industry of consultants has emerged, teaching students how to plan, apply, and pay for college, and providing tutoring, test prep, financial planning, application strategy, and writing support, an "educational industrial complex."[11] These consultants and the media buzz about them have tended to emphasize the complexity and competitive nature of admissions, urging students to write "killer" essays to "win the admissions arms race."[12] As you well know, all of this admissions hype creates even more stress for students. Studies show that stress reduces core attributes of academic effectiveness—memory, confidence, and endurance—and, worst of all, it saps your creativity and the ability to try new things.[13]

Own Your Story, Own Your Life

Write Out Loud takes a different approach, one that fuels creativity, increases your confidence and ability to collaborate, and positions you to thrive not only in admissions, but in college, work, and the rest of your life. The first thing you will learn in *Write Out Loud* is how to "Refresh," to clear out whatever is causing you stress and to approach your essays in a spirit of reflection and curiosity. The three parts of *Write Out Loud* teach you how to use the college process to know yourself better (Part 1: Find); to explore a variety of college and career paths and how each of them fits with your strengths and aspirations (Part 2: Shape); and then use each application essay to connect with colleges that match your strengths and aspirations (Part 3: Perform).

Write Out Loud encourages you to use the college process to take on big questions: What difference do you want to make in the world? Which colleges or universities will prepare you best for the next steps of your life journey? From all of your life experiences, what is your strongest, most compelling story to show colleges who you are and what you will contribute to their communities? *Write Out Loud* walks you through the college application essay process step-by-step, teaching you tools you can use to write personal essays that connect with colleges—and with any community you want to join in the future—and helping you build a portfolio of powerful essays, one by one.

To counter the hype and hysteria surrounding college admissions, I have worked to make the 12 tools in the *Write Out Loud* tool kit accessible and usable. My goal with *Write Out Loud* is to teach a process any student can use to speak powerfully and authentically in his or her college application essays. But the process you learn in *Write Out Loud* applies to much more than college admissions. When you learn how to tell your own story, authentically and in your own voice, not only will you have greater success in college admissions, but you will also have mastered tools that foster leadership in school, work, and life.

The kinds of essays that connect with admissions officers are based on your moments of inspiration, personal growth, and humbly making a difference. Since every student is telling his or her own story—and seeking colleges where his or her unique dreams will thrive—you are not competing with other students. You are having a specific conversation with each college to which you are applying. Even when you and your friends are applying to the same colleges, you can support one another. Each of you is telling your own story and showing colleges who you are and who you want to be.

What Does It Mean to "Write Out Loud"?

To write out loud is to tell your story in a way that makes people pay attention. The best essays bring your voice and presence into the room, so an admissions reader gets to know you and can advocate for you. When everything else is equal, at a school where you are already a strong candidate, your personal essays are your chance to make a case for admitting you. *Write Out Loud* teaches you how to express yourself in writing in a way that makes you present—to perform your stories in a conversational voice, as if you are right there in the room at the admissions office. To write out loud is to be heard as who you are.

A great essay connects with your audience emotionally and lingers with them long after they have finished reading it. I can still remember the best essays I read when I was assessing dozens of applications a day as one of the faculty representatives on the Douglass College Admissions Committee at Rutgers University nearly 20 years ago. A great essay is not magic, and even an off-the-charts essay is not going to get you into a school for which you are not academically qualified.[14]

But there are dozens of cases every day when a great essay makes the difference. From a pool of similar candidates (12 high school quarterbacks who will not play football in college, 15 cellists, or 20 students who all have perfect SATs), the student whose writing speaks directly to the admissions committee, the student who conveys a sense of personal purpose and genuine human connection, is often the one who gets in. As Darryl Jones, Senior Associate Director of Admissions at Gettysburg College, says, "We use the essays to build the soul of the class. I have never once run down the hall to show a colleague that a student has perfect SATs. But a powerful essay—that gets me out of my chair."

Great essays are built on strong and memorable personal stories. When you tell a story, your brain performs a dazzling web of activity: You recall the sensory experience of the story you are telling, the emotions associated with that story are awakened in the present, and based on those memories and emotions you want to take action. All of this happens together in an instant.[15] And—this is why storytelling is so powerful—the person who listens to your story experiences the exact same swirl of brain activity, combining memory, emotion, and action. This mental mirroring is how stories connect us to one another, and how stories enable us to build community. That is why leaders tell stories to galvanize people to collective purpose and how shared cultural stories inform some of our most intimate daily gestures.[16]

When an admissions officer reads an inspiring story, he or she gets to know you and starts to imagine you as part of his or her community. That officer starts to talk about you, advocate for you, and work to admit you. That is what a great story makes a person want to do. It is part of a cycle as old as human culture, a tool kit built into your brain chemistry that everyone can access.

How do you make the connection the human brain craves and seeks through storytelling? *Write Out Loud* will teach you—or rather unleash that power in you. You already know what this book teaches—it is in your brain and connects you with other people. But after SATs, AP exams, and the overall crush of junior year, your creative spark may be hidden under all that other work. In our courses, students often begin approaching their college application essays as if they are writing academic papers: they focus on structure, a thesis statement, introduction, body paragraphs, and conclusion. It is no surprise that this is the case, since many students write first drafts of their college essays in English class, for the same teachers who teach them how to write critical essays.

Since your essays have been evaluated and graded with rubrics developed to assess critical writing, you will often find yourself in the awkward position of looking at essays about yourself *critically*—and looking critically you see what is wrong, at first with the writing and then, in many cases, with yourself. This process is painful to watch and rarely works. Often, the dutiful student writes a well-manicured essay, beautifully written, and just what the teacher wants to hear, but eerily impersonal, distant, and generic sounding. As many great books about college essay writing have shown, there are few universal rules when it comes to writing a standout college application essay.[17] But everyone agrees that impersonal and distant do not work because they just don't forge connections with anyone.

Write Out Loud builds on the fact that college admissions officers are people. Most of them work in admissions because they believe in young people and the transformative power of higher education. Many of them are recent college graduates themselves. Like you, they have passions, dreams, hopes, and ambitions. Like you, they see themselves as self-reliant—or independent, or creative, or a leader.

The key to connecting with admissions officers is to talk to them as if you are telling your story to a friend, face-to-face. When you tell your friend a story, your friend laughs at the funny parts or cries or becomes serious at the tense parts of the story. A story well told triggers your friend to remember another story that relates to yours, and a connection is forged. You tell your friend a story because it matters to you. It is something you want to share. Because it is something that matters to you, it becomes something that matters to him or her. So how do you create that intimacy and trust with a total stranger?

This book teaches you to write as if you are speaking with someone you can trust. *Write Out Loud* takes you through the same exercises we teach in our writing courses and one-on-one coaching. These exercises have been tested and refined with students from a wide range of public and independent schools in the New York area and from all around the United States and around the world—from Oklahoma to Florida and from Geneva, Moscow, and Taipei. *Write Out Loud* is designed to work side by side with a Story To College course, or you can work through the exercises on your own. We invite you to complete each of the exercises, especially the ones that may seem a bit uncomfortable at first. Like a new sport or learning to play a musical instrument, personal essay writing takes practice. You need to exercise different writing muscles separately to achieve the best results overall. And all of that takes time, so be patient with yourself, and don't worry about the results until you have some practice.

Once you learn to use the Moments Method you will be able to develop application essays that you feel really good about without a lot of fuss. And you are much more likely to get into your top choice colleges. But the results of this method go far beyond getting into the college of your dreams. Writing with the power of your spoken voice:

> Connects you with other people
> Improves your writing fluency and confidence
> Enables you to speak with purpose and authority
> Builds habits of mind that prepare you to succeed in college, work, and life

The *Write Out Loud* Promise

Write Out Loud teaches you everything you need to complete all of the writing sections of the new Common Application, as well as applications to other US colleges and universities, all of which use a format similar to the Common Application.

The directions to the new Common Application explain the role of the essay:

> The essay demonstrates your ability to write clearly and concisely on a selected topic and helps you distinguish yourself in your own voice. What do you want the readers of your application to know about you apart from courses, grades, and test scores? Choose the option that best helps you answer that question and write an essay of no more than 650 words, using the prompt to inspire and structure your response.

Write Out Loud teaches you, step-by-step, how to "distinguish yourself in your own voice" in the 650-word Personal Essay on the new Common Application. Chapters 1–4 teach you how to **find** your own unique stories; Chapters 5–8 teach you how to **shape** those stories in response to specific essay and interview questions; and Chapters 9–14 provide strategies to complete your essays and **perform** confidently in writing and in face-to-face interviews. The exercises in each section of *Write Out Loud* enable you to complete a specific aspect of the Personal Essay:

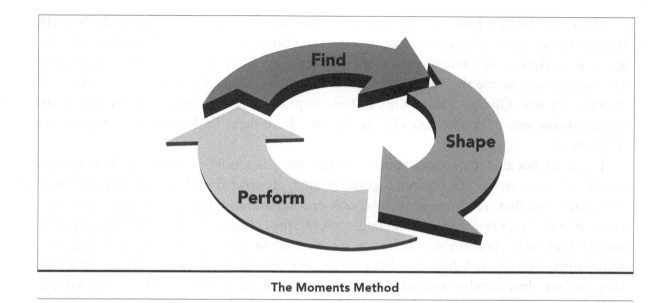

The Moments Method

> In **Part 1: Find** you complete a Story Portfolio.
> In **Part 2: Shape** you complete your first draft of the 650-word Personal Essay.
> In **Part 3: Perform** you edit and complete your essay, so it is ready to submit with your college applications.

College applications include a lot of writing—not just one personal essay but many essays asking you to discuss your experiences and future plans. If you work through the exercises in *Write Out Loud,* one by one, at the end you will have completed every type of question that shows up on the Common Application and other college and university applications and supplements. You will understand how to tackle short-answer questions, the 650-word Personal Essay, and the most common types of supplement essays:

> Defining moments
> Influences
> Issues
> Community
> Academic interests and motivation
> Why this college?
> Anything else you want to tell us?

Write Out Loud teaches a process you can use to write an application essay start to finish—or to approach any other writing assignment. The Moments Method is designed to be easy to learn, use, and share with others. I have included story transcripts and essay drafts by students who used a specific tool to open up something important about themselves—something bigger than just their stories and just that tool. Some of these essays are still rough because I want you to see the pieces and the process that help you achieve successful essays, not just the finished product.

Write Out Loud is based on the concept of "distributed learning." You build new skills, one step at a time, and increase mastery over time through practice and repetition. It's the same as learning a new language, a new instrument, or a new move in your favorite sport: the more you practice the Moments Method the more natural personal storytelling will become for you. Give yourself plenty of time to practice and try different versions of different stories, and over time you will find that you have these tools available whenever you need them.

If you are not able to participate in one of the Story To College courses—either online or on-site—I recommend that you put together a small group of friends to work through *Write Out Loud* together. And in a new notebook or a separate folder on your computer, keep track of everything related to your college process: the colleges you visit, the majors you are considering, and especially new ideas you discover about yourself along the way. When you write things down or tell them to other people, they become real in a way they are not when they are just ideas floating around in your own mind. So the first step of your own Story To College is to put your ideas out in the world, commit to them, and make them real.

Just like our classes, *Write Out Loud* is staged as a dialogue. It is organized around the questions students most often ask: What is a good topic? What is this question asking for? How do I know if my essay is done? Reading someone else's answers and discovering the answers for yourself are two very different types of learning. I invite you to take the slower, sinuous path of self-exploration up the college application mountain. You can treat your essays as another chore to be completed, or you can embrace the challenges, learn new tools, and use the essays as an opportunity to build the story—and person—you bring to college and the rest of your life.

Whenever you have ideas, write them down. In the Further Reading section at the end of each chapter, I include some books and websites you can use to explore the key concepts of *Write Out Loud* in more detail. If you complete *Write Out Loud*, taking charge not only of your essays but your college journey, you will learn skills to walk more confidently on the stage of your own life—in college, work, and everything you do in the future. That is the *Write Out Loud* promise.

The Big Jump

One place that the current hype around college admissions has been useful is in pushing students to identify and pursue their academic and extracurricular passions in high school. The downside: students say no one is allowed to have interests anymore; you must be the CEO of something. This entrepreneurial focus on starting and growing projects of lasting value creates its own pressures and can be more than a bit daunting, but it also allows you to commit to the activities and futures you believe in *right now in the present*. The college admissions process is an opportunity to think strategically about your career path and how you plan to make a difference in the world. Humanity needs more people who have big picture thinking and commitments. The clock is ticking on our planet's survival, and higher SAT scores are not going to save the rain forest or people who are starving halfway across the planet we all share.[18]

In Chapter 11: Raise the Stakes, you learn how to write about issues you are committed to and how you are making a difference in the world right now. In our very first Story To College workshop, we saw that when you put the details of your life into your essays—this can be something as simple as a walk through the park on a snowy day—you experience writing with more confidence and fluency. When you write about what matters to you, it becomes easier for you to write not only your college application essays but other writing as well.[19]

One last word of caution about your college application essays: the rules of engagement that landed you here—getting great grades and test scores and learning to write successful critical essays—is not the skill set you need to write powerful personal essays for your college applications. And it's not the way to succeed in college either. The children's story "The Big Jump" is about a young boy who wins a contest to "jump to the top of the highest building in the land" by jumping up a twisty flight of stairs, one step at a time.[20] The big jump is the one that changes his direction and allows him to see the whole project in a new way.

I encourage you to think about this book as your own big jump, a series of 12 seemingly small lessons that add up to something quite spectacular: the keys to your own kingdom, clarity and confidence about what you bring to colleges, and the ability to share that with others.

If you have read this far, the next step is to give this book to your child. The most important thing you can do to help your child achieve the best college outcome is to encourage your child—early and often and especially when it seems he or she is not ready—to take charge of his or her own college process. That means let your child ask the questions when you visit colleges together, or let your child visit on his or her own. That means let your child decide to prep for the SAT, ACT, both, or neither. That means let your child apply Early Decision or Early Action if he or she is ready, and not if not ready. That means teach your child how to make a spreadsheet with college dates and requirements—or encourage your child to use an online tool such as the one we have at http://storytocollege.com/writeoutloud—but you should *not* fill it out for your child (and no shared passwords).

If my thinking seems to run counter to the trend of parents and consultants managing students' college admissions—it does! The more you hover and nag and manage your child's college process, the less your child will be ready to stand independently after unpacking the suitcases at college. And the more your child's essays sound like you, rather than your child, the less successful your son or daughter will be. So every step of the way, I urge you to stand back, let your child know you trust him or her to manage this important journey and then let your child figure it out.

When it comes to the essays, that means you should not encourage one topic over another, or create a schedule you expect your child to keep (I have seen amazing essays shaped over months of hard work, and equally successful essays come out of nowhere at the last minute), and most of all you should never ever touch the essays, *not even to fix the punctuation*. There's a slippery slope from fixing the punctuation to killing your child's voice and purpose in the essays and turning them into something that sounds flat and generic—too sorted out, too grown-up.

I am convinced—from my work in admissions at Douglass College and reading thousands of student essay drafts through more than 20 years—that the edgy, youthful voice of becoming is far more moving and most often wins out over the voice that has everything tied up in a neat package. Think about it: the people who work in college admissions believe in what college makes possible for young people; they are looking for high school students available for learning and growth. So encourage your child to seek out personal dreams and aspirations in the college process, and especially in the essays. And if your child has a dream he or she has done very little to make real, perhaps you can help with the logistics of getting a few steps closer to that dream in the present. Perhaps you can help your child research courses at your local college or museum, or help brainstorm possible summer jobs or internships, or encourage him or her to spend more time wandering with a sketchbook or camera.

What if your child is someone who seems to have life all figured out? Your child knows he or she wants to be a poet, an engineer, or someone who brings water to Africa. That's great; just know that most students (more than 60 percent) change their course of study once they get to college.[1] If you can learn to be the parent who nurtures your child's independence and helps your child explore his or her own dreams, rather than the parent who provides the dream already complete on a silver platter, everyone will be happier.

There is very little I have not seen in two years of leading Story To College courses. I have seen parents who write the essays for their children. I have seen parents who send their children in with topics they are supposed to write about: the parent's recovery from a long illness, a famous relative, or something else that may or may not be important to the child. I have seen parents who send their children to our courses, and when the child starts to find his or her own voice the parent stops the process, urging the child back to safe, predictable essays once the course is over. Many students describe feeling that their parents do not want to read the essays that they want and need to write: about coming out as a young gay man or lesbian; about wrestling free from some complicated aspect of childhood or family life; about looking at their parents with anything other than adulation and pride.

Your job is to get yourself to the place where you can listen to whatever it is your child needs to say right now. Or, if your child prefers that you not read his or her essays, let that be OK too. I have seen this in many families, and I know personally how hard this can be: my youngest daughter, Eliana, felt so constrained by my criticism—her sense that I wanted her to say things a certain way—that she could not show me anything. The minute she showed me a draft, she lost her way. It was excruciating for both of us. And so I agreed to encourage her in a distant and general way. If your son or daughter asks for that space, I urge you to accept that as a sign that you have done your job. You have nurtured your child's independent spirit; you have made it possible for your child to ask you for what he or she really needs.

Write Out Loud teaches children a process to find their own stories, shape them into successful college application essays, manage the college process, and express their hopes and dreams in ways that are credible in their college application essays and interviews. I have worked with students, parents, English teachers, and college counselors to integrate their questions and concerns into *Write Out Loud*, and I invite you add your voice to the discussion at http://stcstoryup.tumblr.com.

WRITE OUT LOUD

PART 1

FIND

CHAPTER 1

Refresh

*Before you start writing, take a few deep breaths and let go
of your doubts and distractions. Put all of that to the side,
and write with your mind open to whatever you discover.*

Every Story To College class or one-on-one coaching session begins with a version of this exercise that we call Refresh. Why start here? First, there is a growing body of neuroscience research that suggests people who clear their minds daily build more brain cells, experience less mental illness, and discover greater personal resources to work through the obstacles encountered in everyday life.[1] Like broccoli, exercise, and getting enough sleep, daily rituals that free your mind of doubts, distractions, and, especially, self-criticism are surprisingly good for you. Simply put, if you do some sort of meditation regularly you are likely to live longer, enjoy life more, and mess up less.

Second, most students find the college process extremely stressful, and stress shuts down creativity. When you clear out stress, you create a space to engage in the creative work that generates successful college essays. Some people use yoga or exercise as ways to de-stress, and others use prayer. Some use daily journal writing for the same purpose, writing first thing or last thing each day, something I have done since my father bought my first journal in New York after one of his chemotherapy sessions at Memorial Sloan-Kettering Cancer Center.[2]

Why Keep a Journal? and Some Other Helpful Tools

In a study of 678 nuns, the ones who wrote in journals daily lived longer and experienced less depression and less dementia than the ones who did not.[3] So writing a little bit every day—like meditation—helps make your life longer and happier.

A journal helps you succeed in college applications in three important ways—it helps you stay organized, hang on to details (which you will discover are one of the keys to successful application essays), and explore memories and ideas.

> **Stay organized.** If you are like most high school students, your schedule is jam-packed: you rush between school, activities, work, and friends. A journal devoted to your college application process helps you keep track of deadlines, priorities, and ideas you want to explore further. Is everyone telling you to look at Carnegie Mellon? Write yourself a note to research the school later. You definitely want to keep track of all the admissions officers and alumni you talk to, either on campus or when they visit your school, so you can contact them directly to follow up.

> **Hang on to details.** I have heard hundreds of students say that all the colleges they research and visit blur together. That fabulous course the tour guide told you about at Kenyon College will be lost the second you step foot on another campus—whether it is Miami University (in Ohio) or Oberlin. Especially on those crazy days you are shuttling between several different campuses, jot down a few notes about each one. Even something simple, like "way too big; I need a smaller feel," will help bring each of your Why I Want to Go to This College essays to life later.

> **Explore memories and ideas.** If you start to pay attention to the details that pop up when your mind is wandering—maybe something your seventh-grade teacher said about lawyers, or perhaps a rush of associations you have when you run into a homeless person on the subway—you will find unexpected treasures. Great essays always start with your memories and experiences, so when your memories are talking, learn to listen carefully and write down what you remember while it is alive to you in the present.

Wherever you keep your journal—a notebook or a document on your phone or computer—I encourage you to create a separate and special book or folder for all your college work. Call it "(My) STORY TO COLLEGE," and replace "My" with your name. That way you know exactly what it is, and where the journey is going. You can use that journal to complete the exercises in this book, too!

Along with a journal it will be helpful to have a few other things:

> **Pens** (no pencils, no erasers, and for now no "delete" button either)
> **Highlighting markers** in a few different colors (you can do highlighting in most word-processing programs, if you prefer)
> **Sticky notes** to put on your drafts where you want to expand them (or the Notes function online)
> **Recording device** either on your phone or computer or a small, handheld recorder you can throw in your backpack and keep on hand to record ideas and moments that you want to write about later
> **A friend or group of friends** to work through this book and your college application essays together

Studies show that people of all ages are much more likely to persist and complete big projects as part of a group working together.[4] The exercises in Part 2: Shape work really well with a partner who is also going through the college essay process.

"Write it all down," my father said, "the good and the bad." I dutifully listened, capturing it all in my notebook with butterflies and clouds on the cover. When you free write, just letting your thoughts flow without censoring anything, you will come up with many fresh ideas, and you will feel great when you are done! At our Story Up Tumblr site (http://stcstoryup.tumblr.com), we share daily writing themes to get you started, based on research that shows people who write daily produce better writing and win more writing awards.[5] Having a great writing day? We invite you to share that at Story Up too!

Other people restore their emotional equilibrium by immersing in nature or art, so when they are stuck or confused they take time away from work to explore a new place in the outdoors or to wander through their favorite museum (these journeys, by the way, are the start of many great essays; more on that in Chapter 10: Explore Perspectives). The important thing is learning to watch your thoughts. This is called "metacognition," thinking about thinking, a habit of mind that leads to college readiness and college success.[6] Whenever you can take part of your brain out of the moment, stop reacting and begin watching, you are engaging a beautifully complex set of brain functions associated with higher order thinking, leadership, and getting things done.[7] The exercises you practice in this chapter will help you not only to get into your top choice colleges but also to succeed and flourish in college—and in work and everyday life.

Finally, whichever method you choose, a daily discipline for acknowledging and letting go of negative thoughts opens up creativity, generating what scientists of productivity call "flow"; that daily de-junking is like making deposits in the bank of calm for moments in the future when you will need them.[8] And there will certainly be moments in college—and life—when you will want to draw on those reserves of calm confidence! What happens if you forget to refresh for a few days? No worries—just start again when you remember. Do it when you think of it, or when you need it; however it works best for you, in the long run the work pays off.

Ready to give it a try? Here's an exercise you can use to refresh your mind and get ready to start a new project—your college application essays, perhaps, or another project that feels overwhelming and large, like a big rock in your road you cannot move out of the way. Any time you feel that you are not able to focus, or things feel overwhelming or confusing, or everything is too much, try this.

Watching Your Thoughts

Find a quiet place where you will not be disturbed for three minutes. Set a timer (perhaps on your phone or computer) for three minutes. To get started, sit on the ground or in a comfortable chair with your feet on the ground. First, just get comfortable: feel your feet on the ground and experience the energy running through your body. Breathe in to the count of one, two, three; then breathe out to the count of one, two, three. What do you notice? Perhaps you feel your heart beating. Acknowledge your heart, and let that thought go. Perhaps you feel a bit jumpy and find it hard to sit still. Don't worry if the jitters were caused by too much coffee, too little sleep, or something else; just acknowledge them, and on your next exhale let the thought go. And if you are comfortable, I invite you to close your eyes for the rest of the exercise. What do you notice when you close your eyes? Do some of your thoughts or sensations become more heightened? Whatever you are experiencing is totally fine; just acknowledge the thoughts as they arise, and with your next exhale let them go.

For the next few minutes, your only job is to observe what is happening in your body, where your thoughts are wandering, and when they wander, acknowledge where your mind has taken you, and then as you exhale whatever the thoughts, just let them go. Remember: there is no right or wrong. Everyone's mind wanders when they sit quietly; and many people have trouble doing nothing even for 30 seconds. So when the timer goes off, give yourself a smile of acknowledgment for trying something new, open your eyes, and if you had ideas that relate to the college process, write on the following lines or in your journal (or a new document on your computer) as quickly as you can without censoring anything all of your ideas and save them for later. When you write without stopping, you silence your internal critic and find surprising material that would otherwise not make it onto the page. So for at least three minutes, write without your pen leaving the paper or your fingers leaving the keyboard.

Use this exercise for all sorts of stressful moments: right before an interview, or when you are panicking about a test, or when you need to talk to your AP Chemistry teacher about a problem set that has you completely flustered. When you get to college and say to yourself, "Everyone seems smarter than me! They must have made a mistake. I shouldn't really be here," take a deep breath and let all of those doubts and criticisms go. Colleges do not admit people who are not prepared to flourish. When you feel overwhelmed, ask for help and people will teach you how to succeed. If you knew everything already, you wouldn't need college!

But I am getting ahead of myself. My mind is wandering to the future (your future). I need to refresh. . . .

Learning to Doubt Your Doubts

When focusing on the admissions process, and especially writing your application essays, there are some very specific doubts that many students describe as getting in the way of completing—sometimes even starting—their essays. The stress around college admissions has ratcheted up in recent years as colleges receive more and more applications, and the process has become more and more complex and competitive. Many students describe feeling that they are not ready, that they have not done enough, or that what they have done is not "what colleges are looking for."

Here are some of the things that students have said is on their mind at the beginning of the Story To College courses:

> "I have never done this before, and I am freaking out!"
> "There is a lot of information—sometimes conflicting information—and I don't know who to trust."
> "The process is so complicated. Just managing all the pieces feels overwhelming."
> "I am the first person in my family to go to college. The people around me have high expectations, and I have high expectations of myself."
> "My parents seem to be reliving their own college experiences, and that gets in the way of me thinking clearly about my own choices."
> "I've been very successful in high school. It's hard to open up to teachers who have to write letters of recommendation for me."
> "I want schools to know that I am more than just my grades and test scores, but I don't know how to show what that is."
> "I'm not X enough to get into College Y." (X can be anything a student imagines colleges are looking for, and Y is the college that student really wants to attend. I hear this one a lot!)
> "I can't stop comparing myself to other people—including my friends. It's a horrible feeling."
> "I'm just in high school. I have no idea what I want to do with the so-called 'rest of my life.'"

> "I'm afraid that the colleges my parents want me to apply to are not the right ones for me."
> And then there is money . . . many students say some version of "I'm afraid to talk to my parents about where I can afford to go to college" or "I'm afraid that I'll graduate from college saddled with a huge amount of debt."

Financial Aid Basics

Financial aid comes in two types: merit-based and need-based. Merit-based financial aid includes all types of financial support that are based on criteria other than financial need. Different colleges and universities provide a wide variety of scholarships based on academic, athletic, and/or arts achievements. Make sure to check off any box on individual school supplements to indicate that you wish to apply for merit scholarships. Sometimes colleges have an additional essay—either as part of the financial aid application or later—once you are a finalist for top awards. You can use the same process you are learning here to complete compelling personal statements for merit-based financial aid applications. FastWeb (www.fastweb.com) and Cappex (www.cappex.com) are great resources for identifying and learning more about scholarships not based on need.

Need-based financial aid is determined by your own and your family's income, and can be provided by the federal government, the state where you reside, and/or the college or university you attend. If you are a US resident, the Free Application for Federal Student Aid—or FAFSA (www.fafsa.ed.gov)—determines your eligibility for federal financial aid. The FAFSA becomes available January 1 every year, and it is advisable to begin working on it as soon as it is released. You need to fill out a new FAFSA form each year. The federal government provides three types of financial aid: grants, loans, and work study programs.

> Grants do not need to be paid back and are based on your financial need. The Pell Grant Program is the primary type of federal grant, and as of 2013–2014 the maximum award is $5,645 per year.
> Loans are either subsidized or unsubsidized. Subsidized student loans have an interest rate of 6.8 percent, as of July 2013, and unsubsidized loans also have an interest rate of 6.8 percent. Your financial need determines how much you can borrow for your subsidized loan.
> Work study provides part-time jobs to students to help them pay for educational expenses. (For more on work study, see "Three Things to Look For" in Chapter 7.)
> States also provide grants for college students. To find your state's program, visit http://wdcrobcolp01.ed.gov/Programs/EROD/org_list.cfm?category_cd=SGT.
> For a comprehensive explanation of federal financial aid, visit http://studentaid.ed.gov.
> If you are applying early decision, you can fill out the College Scholarship Service (CSS) profile, an alternate financial aid profile (http://student.collegeboard.org/css -financial-aid-profile) that is released before the FAFSA. It is more detailed than the

FAFSA and requires more information. If you get into a school early but do not think it is feasible for you to attend because the aid package is not sufficient for your needs, you can be released from your binding contract.

> Individual colleges and universities also offer merit-based and need-based funding; contact each school's financial aid office for more details.

> For a line-by-line guide to filling out the FAFSA and CSS Profiles, see *Paying for College Without Going Broke*, 13th ed. by Kalman A. Chany with Geoff Martz (New York: Random House, 2012).

> After a school accepts you, it will provide you with a comprehensive financial aid package that breaks down the grants, loans, and work-study opportunities. It will list an expected family contribution: how much you or your family is expected to pay each year based on your income and assets.

> Your aid package is negotiable, but if you want to try to increase your aid package you must act quickly. If you can, use higher financial aid packages you have been offered by other schools for leverage. Make sure you have all the necessary paperwork updated and in order *before* you call your school's financial aid office, and include the name of any admissions officer you have spoken to directly. Be prepared to explain your financial situation in detail, and remember to talk about what you bring to the college community.

> The College Board's Big Future (http://bigfuture.collegeboard.org) is designed to help students with financial aid and offers checklists, questions for financial aid officers, and informational videos.

> A variety of private organizations offer independent scholarship awards for college. Sites for finding these opportunities include: Zinch (www.zinch.com), Big Future (https://bigfuture.collegeboard.org/scholarship-search), College Greenlight (www.collegegreenlight.com/), and FastWeb (www.fastweb.com).

Maybe you are experiencing some of these concerns, or maybe you have others. We list them here because we want you to know that you are not the only student experiencing bumps along the road to college. For most students the process is challenging, confusing, and stressful.

Whatever you have on your mind, it is likely that other students—your friends as well as total strangers who are in the midst of the college process—are experiencing similar doubts and fears. To the extent that you can identify and work through your fears—by answering the questions that need to be answered (like money and which colleges are a good fit for you), and letting your doubts dissolve, you will have a lot more fun in the college process, and you are also much more likely to achieve the outcomes you want.

Since you bought this book—or your parents or school bought it for you—to complete your college application essays, the next two exercises will help you focus on your college application journey. Did you notice that I used "your" (the college process is not anyone else's; it is yours to define) and "journey" (how you get there is just as important as where you end up)? I invite you to use the next two exercises to explore the stories you have been told about college and the stories you tell yourself.

EXERCISE 2

My Story To College

Find a place that is quiet and where you will not be disturbed for five minutes. Set a timer for five minutes. Sit on the ground or in a comfortable chair with your feet on the ground. If you are comfortable doing so, I invite you to close your eyes. Take a couple of breaths to settle down, check in with yourself, and get comfortable with your breath flowing in and out. Breathe in slowly to the count of three, and breathe out slowly to the count of three. Do this a few times, and each time let go of anything you are holding on to—any doubts or fears, any judgments about yourself or other people.

Let all that go out your feet into the ground and open up a space in your mind and heart—imagine your head opening up and expanding to who you are going to be and what you are going to do in college. Imagine yourself there—perhaps you have visited colleges, and there is one that is at the top of your list; if you haven't visited colleges yet, no worries—just imagine that you are there, wherever "there" is. What classes will you take? What will you do when you are not in class? What color is your dorm room, and what will you say when you meet your roommate? What will you do in college that you have never done before? Spend time imagining yourself in college. At the end of the college process, where is it that you want to be? And slowly, when you are ready, open your eyes and on the next page or in your journal or in a new document write down what you saw, what you said, and what you did when you imagined yourself in college.

Now that you have a picture of where you are going—not just the name of the college, but the courses, the activities, and what you will do as a member of that college community—you can take specific steps to get there. As you continue through this book, you are likely to discover other things you want for yourself in college. I encourage you to write them all down. Thoughts about the future sometimes come in an unexpected rush, when you least expect them. Get in the habit of writing them down while they are fresh, before you get busy with something else and forget them.

When you are considering which colleges to apply to, look for colleges where you will make a meaningful contribution and where you will begin accomplishing your dreams. Many students have a hard time sorting out their own college hopes and dreams from those of their relatives and friends. Sometimes advice from parents and teachers can be extremely helpful; other times it can be overwhelming. The next exercise is designed to help you clear out the clutter of other people's expectations to explore your own Story To College.

EXERCISE 3

My Family's Story To College

Find a quiet place where you will not be disturbed for 10 minutes. Set a timer for 10 minutes. Sit on the ground or a comfortable chair with your feet on the ground. Close your eyes, and take a few breaths, checking in with yourself and getting comfortable with your breath flowing in and out. Breathe in slowly to the count of three, and breathe out slowly to the count of three. Each time you breathe in, think about someone who has told you something about college, and when you breathe out, let that person and their ideas go. Remember, you can always come back to their ideas later; you aren't saying or doing anything to them or their ideas, you are just clearing a space to do your own thinking. Repeat this process, and with each exhale let go of other people's words and ideas about the college process. That college where your family has gone for generations? Breathe out and let it go. Your father wants you to be an engineer? Breathe out and let that go. Your English teacher told you, "You are the best writer in your class." Hard as it may seem, on your next breath, let that one go too. Just open up a space—imagine a field you will plant with your own ideas as seeds—that is open and available, and when you open your eyes, on the following lines or in your journal write down what you see yourself doing there. Be as specific as possible, and list at least 20 things.

What Will I Do in College?

1. _____
2. _____
3. _____
4. _____
5. _____
6. _____
7. _____
8. _____
9. _____
10. _____
11. _____
12. _____
13. _____
14. _____
15. _____
16. _____
17. _____
18. _____
19. _____
20. _____

Some of the ideas you found in these exercises may be helpful, and they may reveal influences and aspirations you want to describe in your application. You will work with these influences in Chapter 3: Transform Scripts to Stories, and in Chapter 10: Explore Perspectives. For now, just write down what you find, and give yourself permission to have your own ideas and take charge of your own college admissions process—and especially the stories you tell in the personal essays.

The first question almost every student asks is "What topic makes a good college application essay?" Another version of this question is "I just can't figure out what to write about. Nothing seems right. Can you help me find a good topic?" There are a number of books that begin by answering that question, describing what you should and should not write about and showing you examples of successful essays on various topics.[9]

Over and over, I have found that approach—looking for someone else's idea of a great topic and writing to their specifications—does not help. Often, being told what to write about prevents students from writing their best essays. Whether a college counselor says, "You need to write an essay that makes you sound more intellectual," or a parent says, "You shouldn't write about your sister's mental illness," once you start down that path, most students find it really hard to get out of the mind-set of writing to someone else's definitions of what makes a "good essay." In contrast, the Moments Method teaches you a process to find your own most important stories, and then to shape those stories in response to the questions asked on different college applications. Try to be patient with yourself while you learn the process and the tools to find your stories and shape them into successful essays that connect with admissions readers. Most students explore a variety of personal stories before they find the ones that work best for them in college admissions. The next three chapters give you exercises to find your own stories, so you learn the process and have lots of material to work with in your essays.

My AP French teacher, Mrs. O'Neill, who told breathtaking stories about serving in the French Resistance during World War II, used to say, "The French word for *essay* comes from the verb *essayer*, 'to try.' Keep trying and you will find the way." To find your way you will almost definitely need to explore some of your life's stickier moments, times when you were not the star student, times when you made mistakes and learned from them. That is how life works. You do not learn life's most important lessons from a book; you learn them in what my father called the "school of hard knocks." You may find yourself remembering stories that you have never told anyone—moments from your own life you think for one reason or another you are not *supposed* to tell. The idea, again and again, is to clear out your doubts and self-criticism whenever you sit down to write, and let yourself explore what you find in the stories of your own life. Self-criticism, as well as criticism of others, cuts off the spontaneous flow of ideas you need to be able to generate powerful essay topics.

Guilt-Free Zone

The next exercise is based on something that happened around my own kitchen table when Zach and Talia, my two older children, were in middle school. It was just after September 11, 2001. My marketing business had lost a lot of money, and I was about to sell it. My husband's parents were both sick with terminal illnesses, and our best friend's daughter had pancreatic cancer. I would come home from work and cook something quickly. Then we'd all eat in silence. Several nights in a row there were winks and giggles between the kids.

"What's going on?" I asked. Silence.

On the third night, before I cleared the dishes I said, "I declare the dinner table a Guilt-Free Zone. Anything you say here stays here. No one can tell anyone else, and no one gets in trouble for what they say honestly around the dinner table." And then they told me who was kissing whom behind the gym after lunch.

In the summer of 2010 when Charles Inniss, Ben White, and I were teaching a Narativ workshop for high school students at Lehman College, CUNY, there was a student named Winston who rarely spoke. He often came to class late, hungry, and tired. Students were telling stories about their neighborhoods. When it was Winston's turn, he quietly started to tell a story, but no one could hear him. Then he said, "I can't. I just can't."

I told the story about my kids and the Guilt-Free Zone and said, "I want you to consider this class an extension of my kitchen table. This class is a Guilt-Free Zone." And Winston went on to tell a story about a time his friends had harassed the owner of a Chinese takeout restaurant in their neighborhood, throwing packets of mustard and sweet and sour sauce on the floor and laughing at her broken English. As the old woman was chasing the boys out of her store, Winston turned to her and said, "I'm sorry for what my friends did. I'm really sorry." But she could not understand his English and waved her arms at him to leave.

Here is an exercise to create your own Guilt-Free Zone for college essay writing.

Guilt-Free Zone

Find a quiet place where you will not be disturbed. Set your timer for 10 minutes. Sit on the ground or a comfortable chair with your feet on the ground. Close your eyes, and spend a minute or so checking in with yourself and getting comfortable with your breath flowing in and out. Breathe in slowly to the count of three, and breathe out slowly to the count of three. As you breathe in and out, imagine you are a mountain and in front of you is a lake. All of your past experiences are falling like tiny pebbles into the lake and sinking slowly to the bottom. And as you breathe in, let yourself remember things that have happened to you or things you have done. It doesn't matter whether these things worked or not, or whether you've told anyone else or not; and it doesn't matter whether what you did or what happened to you was right or wrong. Whatever you remember just let your memories drop like pebbles into the lake. You are the strong and enduring mountain, and you are just watching. And then see what else appears, and let that pebble sink with the others into the lake of your experience, your learning, and your life up until now. And when the timer goes off, open your eyes and write down each of the pebbles, without guilt or fear, just exactly as you remember them.

The exercises in this chapter enable you to watch your own thoughts, without judgments or criticism. Remember: you want to create in yourself an observer, not a traffic cop, and certainly not a crime scene investigator looking for evidence that something in you is broken or wrong. The college process may show you parts of yourself that you are not so proud of—the class you skipped in ninth grade, or the time you watched someone get hurt and did nothing, or the time you shoplifted with your friends—whatever it is, if you find something that bothers you, accept it as part of your past and commit to change your actions in the present.

If you have done these exercises, even one of them, you have learned **Tool #1: Refresh**. Whenever you experience doubts and criticisms crowding out clear thinking, create a safe space, a "Guilt-Free Zone" where you are in charge. You are free to explore whoever you want to be in college and which stories you want to tell in your college application essays. Some stories may conjure up stuff you do not want to talk about or deal with in your applications, and that is fine. Or you may not be sure if they are "right" for application essays. Try not to worry about that for now either. The first third of *Write Out Loud* is about finding your stories—the more stories you find, the more material you have to work with in the actual essays. It is your application process, and they are your essays. In later chapters you will figure out which stories go where (including which ones stay in your notebook). For now, just give yourself permission to explore what is actually in your past and present to write about. When doubts and criticism rear their ugly faces, just acknowledge them gently and then put them to the side.

One final word—let's call it the *valedictory*, from the Latin word for "last word." Remember to give yourself the prize: imagine you have been admitted to the college of your dreams (see it, feel it, experience it), and work backward from there, doing the things that the person who wins the prize does every day.[10] Whenever your mind wanders, bring yourself back to this space of winning. Before you write—whatever you are writing—take the time to free your mind of doubts and distractions, press the "refresh" button like you do on your computer when the cache gets clogged, and write with an open and expansive frame of mind.

Further Reading

Cameron, Julia. *The Artist's Way*. New York: Penguin Group, 1992.

Csikszentmihalyi, Michaly. *Flow: The Psychology of Optimal Experience*. New York: Harper Perennial, 1991.

Han, Thich Nhat. *Being Peace*. Berkeley: Parallax Press, 2005.

Story Up! Tumblr: http://stcstoryup.tumblr.com.

Thoreau, Henry David. *Walden (Or, Life in the Woods)*. New York: Dover Publications, 1995.

Trafton, Anne. "The Benefits of Meditation." *MIT News*, May 4, 2011. http://web.mit.edu/newsoffice/2011/meditation-0505.html.

CHAPTER 2

Build a Bridge

Education is all a matter of building bridges.

—RALPH ELLISON[1]

Stones Across the River: A Parable

Just when you think you are standing in a secure place, something changes. In an instant you feel the water lapping around your feet. You need to jump from the stone you know to another stone, one that is different and seems infinitely far away. The more comfortable the old stone, the harder it can be to leave. You may be prepared or not. You may be a swimmer or not. You may own a boat, or you may not. But when the waters come, you have to leave. You gather up what you have and leap across the water—or into the water—and aim for a place you have never been before. Once you are in the water you see what was there all along: tools to build a bridge; smaller stones where you can stand along the way; and people who will help you swim across. But you rarely see those new tools and new people until you leap from a place that is secure into a new place, a bit foreign, strange, and unknown.

Your Story from the Past to the Future

Today, right now, you are creating your story to somewhere. You are taking everything you have done in the past and making a credible case—a bridge—from your past to your future. For most students, college is a big step, and college applications are the first time you need to show total strangers why they should believe in you and advocate for you based on what you have already done.

College application essays are your chance to show colleges who you will be in their communities by revealing parts of your character that do not show up in your school and

REFRESH

Stones Across the River

Write about a time you took a leap into something unknown. Set a timer and keep your pen moving or your fingers typing for three minutes or more.

extracurricular records. Great admissions essays are not about grades or test scores; they are not about academic or athletic or artistic achievements (those are all things that are important and included in other parts of your application). Great essays reveal who you are as a person today, how you got to this place, and where you are committed to going in the future.

Since you will need to build this type of bridge again and again—a story that gets you from college to your first job or graduate school; from one job to the next; from one country to another; from one relationship to another—the tools you are learning for the college application process in *Write Out Loud* are transferable skills you will use again in the future. But for now you are building a bridge from high school to college. The stories you tell in your application essays create that bridge.

In this chapter you build your own bridge from the things you have done in the past to the person you want to be in college—and beyond college. You will make a case for the type of person you will be and what you will contribute in the future based on what you have already done in the past and what you are doing right now in the present. In order to build that bridge and make that case, you will bring together the things you have done that are relevant—not just from school but from every area of life. Then you will focus on the details of where you are going, replacing general ideas like "I've always wanted to be a doctor" with something very specific to you, such as, "I am fascinated with how the human brain works. I want to study neuroscience and ethics to ensure that we use science wisely and in ways that foster community."

Remember the rocks and the river? Don't expect yourself to get there all at once! This process takes time; it includes self-exploration as well as learning what different colleges look like, what different careers look like, plus sifting and sorting and thinking seriously about what is a good fit for you. The first step is putting all of your ideas on paper so you can look at them one by one.

EXERCISE 1

My Life Story

Write your life story. Start with "I was born . . ." and keep writing without your pen leaving the paper or fingers leaving the keyboard for 10 minutes or longer. As you get closer to the present, try to slow down and include as many events and details as you can remember from the past three years.

The Bridge

You will draw on elements of your life story in your college application essays, and you will add other events and details as you think of them. The next exercise starts to connect the dots between your life in the past, your life right now, and your life as you start to plan for it in college. We call this exercise The Bridge.

The Bridge is a tool to explore the unique experiences and dreams you bring to college and to consider which colleges are a good fit for you. The Bridge encourages you to think about the connections between your past and your future. Lots of great essays flow from this chart; so take your time, and feel free to come back to it when you think of more ideas. Ideas may bubble up when you are working on something else, so you may want to bring *Write Out Loud* or your College Journal in your backpack, and when you remember important moments from your past or hopes for your future take a second and jot them down.

The boxes on the left side of The Bridge—Commitments, Ambitions, and Aspirations—are what you will do and be in college and beyond. Here are the kinds of things you want to put in each of these boxes:

> **Commitments:** What is the purpose and direction of college for you? What can you be counted on to contribute to your college community? How do you reveal those commitments in your life today?

> **Ambitions:** What do you see yourself doing in college, in work, and in life? There is a lot more to college than courses; in fact, much of the most important learning in college takes place outside the classroom. What steps will you take in college toward your future career? What do you want to do in college besides take courses? Do you imagine internships, community service, or running the student government? This is your chance to plan your future, adding as much specific detail as possible, and eventually looking for colleges where you will be able to build the skills you need to fulfill your boldest dreams.

> **Aspirations:** When a college invests in you, what bigger vision is it investing in? When your life is over and you look back, what difference will you have made? Around what challenge—global or local—are you engaged and making a difference? Don't have a "big so what" in your life? Check out *High Noon: 20 Global Problems and 20 Years to Solve Them* by the former head of the World Bank in Europe.[2] As a human community we are several years into his 20 years, and the challenges he describes could all benefit from your creativity. To talk meaningfully about an issue, in either an essay or interview, you need to show where that issue intersects with you; once you see that there is a challenge, what do you do about it? We'll talk more about how to write essays about issues in Chapter 11: Raise the Stakes. For now identify where you want to make a difference, and start making that difference today. The difference between *ambitions* and *aspirations* is important. Ambitions are what you want to do (I want to be a doctor); aspirations are what difference you want to make (I want to cure cancer).

The Bridge

What are the most important things you want colleges to know about you? In each section of The Bridge, write down at least 10 specific details from your past or your future. The six boxes are described in more detail in the text.

COMMITMENTS

What difference do you want to make in the world?

AMBITIONS

What do you plan to study? What else will you do in college? What are your plans after college?

ASPIRATIONS

What is the purpose of your life?

ACTIVITIES

What activities do you enjoy?

ATTRIBUTES

What words would you use to describe yourself?

INFLUENCES

Which people have shaped who you are today? Which works of art, literature, or science have shaped you as a person?

Think about the connections between what you want to do for yourself and what you want to do in the world. For instance, you might think "I want to study law" (ambition), "so I can run for local office and build a safer community" (aspiration). You may not have thought like this before; take some time, do some research, and let yourself imagine different futures. The more you can show colleges who you will be and what you will do—in college and in life—the better you will connect with them, and help yourself be noticed in the admission pool.

In the next three boxes—Activities, Attributes, and Influences—you want to be very specific about what you did and who influenced you to help you become who you are today:

> **Activities:** These are things you have done. Not just school and extracurricular activities, but family life, jobs, that summer with your grandparents, things you do when you are alone, and everyday things with your family and friends. When you travel what do you do in other places? For instance, if you were part of a religious group that traveled to Costa Rica to repair a school, what did you do that was uniquely your own? Be very specific: it may have been one conversation in Spanish with one girl your age from the community. Write down where you were sitting, what the weather was like, and the exact words each of you said. What are your hobbies? Your passions? What do you do just for fun?

> **Attributes:** These represent who you are at the core, what people know they can count on you for. Get past the obvious (e.g., ambitious and hardworking). Some attributes—the ones related to school especially—may be better for your teachers and coaches to describe. What can you add to the picture that your teachers may not talk about? Asking yourself, "What's the most important thing people may not know about me?" is one way to start exploring that question. The important attributes may be those you take for granted. Perhaps you are the person who makes sure everyone gets along; maybe you take a back seat and make sure everyone wins, rather than tooting your own horn. In the ebb and flow of high school life, awards and recognition often go to people who are more outwardly competitive, so make sure you show people that you are a leader in a different way, someone who can be counted on to build and maintain community in college.

> **Influences:** Who has had an impact on you and touched your life in a way that made a difference? List them here, and be very specific about what you learned from them. In Chapter 3: Transform Scripts to Stories you will explore these influences further, and in Chapter 10: Explore Perspectives you will learn how to talk about them in college application essays that ask about influences. If there are places in your life where you have influenced others or made a lasting impression, list those too: a time you started something, perhaps, or moved a project in an important new direction.

Connect the Past with the Future

You make your future dreams palpable in college application essays by showing what you have done in the past and how it has shaped you. For each essay, for each college, you use your past experiences to show admissions readers who you will be as a member of that college community. Before you can connect your dreams with colleges in a way that is genuine and meaningful, you need to explore what they really are.

You may be thinking, "I have solid grades and test scores, why do I need to do all this extra work?" Perhaps you know students who were leaders of their class in high school and failed to get into colleges they were most excited about. Chances are they did not give colleges reasons to believe in them. But what if strong grades and great test scores assured you would get into the college of your dreams (which is how college admissions decisions are made in many other countries)? College application essays are not just transactional; they are not just about getting into college. The college application process, and especially writing the essays, is a chance to construct your *character*, a chance to reveal to colleges (and your parents and college counselor, and maybe even yourself) what matters to you.

Or maybe you are thinking, "I don't know what I want to do." Honestly, most high school students do not think about this so much. Or they think about it constantly, obsessively, but it's all in their heads. I am inviting you to make your dreams real, to write them down, and to start acting on them.

Or perhaps you feel like you have not done very much that matters. There's always time to change that. If you could do one thing differently today, what would it be? It could be as simple as helping your mom make dinner when she gets home from work exhausted, or taking out the garbage because your sister is at play rehearsal. Get in the habit of doing those small everyday acts for others, and before you know it, you will have lots of new stories to tell in your college applications. Taking out the garbage, you run into a skunk, or a rat perhaps, depending on where you live, or maybe you have a conversation with the old man who lives next door and that begins a new friendship.

The Moments Method is not about what happens in your head, but what you do in the world. What happened in your life the day after you experienced for a brief second the feeling that all people are connected? What did you do or say the first time your religious faith was tested? When you find a day with nothing in it, how do you fill it?

Most students' "go to" essays are quite predictable—sports victories, creative inspiration, or hard work and achieving what you were trying to achieve. These essays are quite formulaic, and they are not very interesting. In Chapter 3 you will learn how to branch out from these very predictable topics with **Tool #3: Transform Scripts to Stories**. Here I invite you to journey back into your own experience to build a more powerful foundation for your essays and a more powerful foundation for your future. I encourage you to go beyond the usual—the things many people can say, or the things you routinely say—and explore some new territory, both in your past and in your future.

The next exercise shows you how to use The Bridge to connect with the college admissions officers who read your application.

The Most Important Thing

W hat is the most important thing you want colleges to know about you? First write down a few sentences, almost like a meditation.

_____

_____

_____

_____

_____

Then take some time and craft one sentence of 10 words or less.

_____

_____

Then, distill that sentence down to one word, the most important word, something that characterizes and defines you. Write down under Attributes in The Bridge exercise the one word that you want colleges to know about you.

_____

Now think of 10 or more moments from your past or present that show that attribute— 10 things you have done, moments when you grew or learned or changed in some fundamental way, or people who have helped to shape that attribute in you.

1. _____

2. _____

3. _____

4. _____

5. _____

6. _____

7. _____

8. _____

9. _____

10. _____

Take your time and list as many moments as you can think of that show that one attribute to other people. As you explore that one attribute, you will probably think of other important attributes. Your hopes and dreams may become visible, too. Write down whatever you think of during this exercise, but stick with that first attribute—or another one that feels more compelling to you—and find 10 moments that reveal that attribute to others. You will discover that these exercises start to get interesting around number 8—and a bit giddy and unpredictable around number 13—so keep going, writing down as many moments as you can think of that reveal each thing you want colleges to know about you.

Work back and forth. Ask yourself how you can bridge from the past to the future: Where in my current experience are the seeds of what I plan to do in the future? Can't find seeds in the present? Create them in some small act you take today. Planning to be an engineer? Google "famous engineers" and you open up a world of experience about what engineers have done in the past and what they are doing today. There are websites where you can read their stories, and learn how they see engineering evolving in the future. You can find nearly anything online if you put in a bit of research time. And all of that research, all of those details, will make a huge difference in the vitality and credibility of your college application essays.

Then try it the other way, building a bridge back from the future: What have my pivotal life experiences taught me, and what do they suggest about where I am going and what I want to do? Do you feel like you lack major experiences and influences? Many students feel that way. You can seek out more experiences by connecting with people who have done what you want to do. Even students just a couple years older than you, who have gone to the types of colleges you are looking for, can open up a world of new information. Who else in your own community can provide advice and contacts for your journey?

Share What You Have Done

Simple human acts and dreams are what succeed most in college application essays—and many other parts of life. Even when you win the Intel science competition, the fact that you won is less important than what you have done: an experiment that reveals something new about the world that we didn't know before (and that's fantastic)! Even more than what you have won—and even if you are the person who comes in second or you do not win any outward awards—what difference does it make that you took on this project and discovered something new?

Sometimes we are not the best judges of our own characters. We tend to take for granted our unique strengths, the things that are most sturdy and enduring about ourselves. In this next exercise you reach out to important people in your life, to learn how they see you and to gather up the stories and moments that they treasure in you.

Community Voices

First make a list of the five people you are going to interview.

1. _____

2. _____

3. _____

4. _____

5. _____

Schedule time to connect with at least five people from different parts of your life, and write those times here and also in your calendar or planner.

Then prepare questions that will allow them to talk about you. Here are some examples:

> What do you value about me? What can you count on me for?
> Was there ever a time that you saw me make a difference? What do you remember?
> If you could change one thing about me, what would it be?

Your job in this exercise is to listen and learn how others see you. Feel free to make up your own questions. What do you most want to know about how people see you? If you record these conversations—on your phone or computer—you can listen better, knowing you can go back and listen again later for the details. So turn on your recorder, thank the person for his or her time, and then ask questions to start the conversation. Let each person say whatever is on that person's mind, and when something unexpected is said, ask for more information. You can think of yourself as a reporter interviewing experts. When you go back later and listen, note the exact words each person says in quotation marks, so you can include their words in your essays. (See "Grammar Rules for Dialogue" in the sidebar Working with Quotations in Chapter 7: Focus Out.)

Interview #1

NAME: _____

After you listen to the recording of this interview, write down three to five things the person said in exactly his or her words that you might want to use in college application essays.

_____

_____

_____

_____

_____

Interview #2

NAME: _____

After you listen to the recording of this interview, write down three to five things the person said in exactly his or her words that you might want to use in college application essays.

_____

_____

_____

_____

_____

Interview #3

NAME: _____

After you listen to the recording of this interview, write down three to five things the person said in exactly his or her words that you might want to use in college application essays.

_____

_____

_____

_____

_____

Interview #4

NAME: _____

After you listen to the recording of this interview, write down three to five things the person said in exactly his or her words that you might want to use in college application essays.

_____

_____

_____

_____

_____

Interview #5

NAME: _____

After you listen to the recording of this interview, write down three to five things the person said in exactly his or her words that you might want to use in college application essays.

_____

_____

_____

_____

_____

In Exercise 4: Community Voices you may have discovered how people from different parts of your life notice slightly different things when asked the same question. Perhaps you asked, "What do you value most about me?"

> A friend may say, "The way you smile when I tell you about my accomplishments."
> Your mom may remember, "You love to cook. When you came home from National Outdoor Leadership School, you made me sandwiches to take to work."
> And a teacher may add to the picture, "You ask great questions. You admit when you are confused. That puts other students at ease. And it helps me figure out where I need to focus so others will understand too." The teacher who knows you that well, by the way, will be able to write a great recommendation for you; tuck that piece of information away for later!

Invite each person to share stories about you. If they have known you for a long time, how have they seen you change over the years? If you go to a small school perhaps there is a teacher you had in seventh grade and then again in high school. Or perhaps there is a neighbor or the owner of a bodega on the corner who has known you and your family for many years. What have they seen? Was there something unusual about the way you dressed—for example, the owners of our local bakery remember my daughter Talia as the girl who wore a Belle dress the entire summer after *Beauty and the Beast* came out. You learn a lot about Talia's character from that one detail, right? Those are the kinds of things you are asking your community to help you remember and piece together.

We all have important aspects of our character we tend to take for granted. We sometimes assume it is easy to do what we are best at; we imagine everyone can do it. Your job in college application essays is to find those things that are unique to you. Look for stories that reveal them first to the people who know you best and then to colleges. For instance, to the person who makes everyone get along, it is second nature; that person may not even notice the absence of fighting that he or she has generated. The objectives of the last exercise were to help you see your own character from the outside, and to find specific moments that reveal that character to others. Some of the people you talk to may also have influenced you in significant ways. In Chapter 3: Transform Scripts to Stories and Chapter 10: Explore Perspectives, you will learn how to write about influences. For now just write down what they said, especially the specific words and details that stick with you and remind you of your best self, your big dreams.

Remember with The Bridge you can start either in the future—where you are going—and build a bridge to get there; or you can explore what is most powerful and moving in your past and present and explore where that takes you. The next exercise explores The Bridge from another angle, with an eye to what type of work you may want to do in the future, and what you might study in college to get there.

What You Bring to the Game

Look at the diagram with the three overlapping circles, and write down at least 10 things in each category.

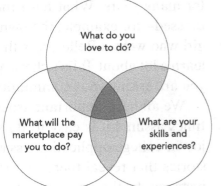

Your Sweet Spot

What Do You Love to Do?

1. _____
2. _____
3. _____
4. _____
5. _____
6. _____
7. _____
8. _____
9. _____
10. _____
_____
_____

What Are Your Skills and Experiences?

1. _____
2. _____
3. _____
4. _____
5. _____

6. _____

7. _____

8. _____

9. _____

10. _____
_____
_____

What Will the Marketplace Pay You to Do?

1. _____

2. _____

3. _____

4. _____

5. _____

6. _____

7. _____

8. _____

9. _____

10. _____
_____

In *Good to Great*, author Jim Collins uses this diagram to describe where companies will flourish best.[3] This model of business excellence can be applied to individuals as well. Exercise 5: What You Bring to the Game is an opportunity to explore those three circles one by one. For each category, think of as many things as you can—aim for 10 or more, since that is often where interesting ideas begin to emerge. And while you are making your lists, ask yourself these questions:

> Are there things I loved to do when I was younger but for some reason gave up?

> Is there anything that I am so good at that it takes up all my time and keeps me from trying other things that I am interested in but never seem to get around to?
> Is there anything so much a part of who I am, something I am so good at that I take it for granted?

When you are completing the circle about the marketplace, consider what types of work in college (not just classes and jobs, but activities, service, and internship opportunities) will help you experience the ups and downs of those professions, almost like an apprenticeship for a trade in earlier times.[4]

There may be activities you do a lot that seem a bit frivolous, or not serious enough to share with colleges—like making cupcakes or collecting the fortunes from fortune cookies. Just capture what it is you actually do, however you really spend your time, so you can explore what these everyday experiences reveal about who you are and how you make a difference in the world around you. Here are a few examples:

> Let's say you love children and have done a lot of babysitting. You might think about being a teacher or a guidance counselor or someone who runs after-school programs for children. So far that's pretty obvious. How do you get past the obvious? Ask yourself: What did I enjoy most about babysitting—was it helping kids with their homework? Teaching them how to make a video? Cooking? Talking to the kids or their parents? Or maybe you just wanted the kids to go to bed so you could work on your homework? Be honest about that too!
> Or perhaps you were your class president junior year—a fact that will show up on your activities résumé, so just being president is not a great essay topic. What did you love about being president? What did it teach you that you will bring with you to college? Did you take on new initiatives? Did you get other students past a conflict to a place of compromise? Did you broker something between students and the administration? These are all important attributes of leadership but very different from one another. When you say you are a leader, what type of leader are you, and which specific moments or experiences reveal your unique leadership commitments to others?
> Or maybe you are the quiet student who demands little attention, but behind the scenes you do many things that help other people. How can you show what you are doing that may go unnoticed? What does your quiet approach reveal about who you are and what you will bring to college and professional life?

See what you discover about yourself from exploring each of your jobs or extracurricular activities in this way: What did I love? What skills did I gain? Which college majors or careers overlap with the things I love to do and where I have experience?

Perhaps you have no idea what the market will pay for. Start to explore that too.[5] Ask people in professions you are considering if you can follow them for a day (most people love to give advice); visit blogs and websites of business leaders and innovators in the areas where your passions and strengths overlap. Explore how you can build a career around what you love, figuring out how to monetize your passions and commitments.

Perhaps you are saying to yourself, "This is a lot of work! Do I really need to take the time to do this?" Imagine the difference between an interview where the person reveals his or her commitment with specifics—for example, "I shadowed a nuclear physicist at the state college, and then I sat in on his class" or "My mom forced me to go to Engineering camp, so I would know what I was committing my life to, and I became obsessed with the medical applications of nanotechnology"—and the person who says very general things like, "I've always been interested in science." Which one of those students would you admit to your college? If you take the time to show who you are and what you bring to whichever college is lucky enough to have you as part of their community, it will also clarify which colleges are a good fit for you.

Types of Colleges

There are more than 4,000 four-year colleges in the United States and hundreds more in other countries. Here are two ways you can organize different types of colleges as you begin to explore your college options.

WHAT IS THE FOCUS?
> **Liberal Arts College:** The first and most well-known colleges in the United States were designed along this model. From the Latin word *collegium*, for a group of equals, the focus at liberal arts colleges is small-group undergraduate teaching and collaborative learning across a wide range of subjects. Classes tend to be small and support services well integrated into community life. You can probably walk or ride your bike from one end of campus to the other.
> **Research University:** Research universities tend to be large and multifaceted, with thousands of students and multiple campuses. They often have graduate schools of medicine, law, business, or engineering, as well as undergraduate schools or programs. Faculty members are responsible for research as well as teaching and tend to be less involved in the everyday life of undergraduates. Advanced graduate students teach some of the introductory courses. Large universities often have robust counseling and career services, but it will be up to you to find them.
> **Specialized:** These are often newer programs with a very specific professional focus. For instance, Olin specializes in engineering, Babson in business (Olin and Babson have an innovative joint program in engineering and entrepreneurship), and Fashion Institute of Technology, aka "FIT," in New York trains students for careers in the fashion industry. Your core classes will be focused on learning a professional skill set and gaining experience and credentials in your chosen field.

WHO GOVERNS AND WHO PAYS?
> **Private:** Private colleges and universities come in many different types and sizes. While they are responsible to a variety of state and federal laws governing education, each has its own unique mission, leadership, and fiscal structure.

> **Public:** The major state universities were started under the Morrill Acts of 1862 and 1890 to educate citizens in practical subjects such as agriculture, physical science, and engineering. While even public universities depend on fund-raising from private sources, the large state university systems remain committed to educating the widest range of people from their state. They are governed through specific state laws and annual funding from the state legislature.

To start exploring colleges that are a good fit for you, visit Big Future (www.bigfuture.org), Noodle (www.noodle.org), and Zinch (www.zinch.com).

EXERCISE 6

Connect to Your Colleges

If you have not started researching specific colleges, this exercise is your chance to explore different colleges and different types of colleges in depth. If you live close enough to visit in person, try to see different types of campuses, in order to get a better sense of what different colleges offer. If you are not able to visit in person, many colleges have virtual tours online allowing you to learn about many more colleges than you need to visit.[6] For each college you research, find at least five very specific things—such as classes, professors, or activities—that you can imagine doing there. The following chart will help you keep track of the details.

1. Choose three colleges that interest you.

_____

_____

_____

2. Spend time on each of the three college's websites and research three aspects of each college that interest you.

College 1: _____

_____

_____

_____

College 2: _____

_____

_____

_____

College 3: _____

_____

_____

_____

3. For each college, select one of those aspects and write down moments that show how that aspect connects to you. Remember, you will be at college for four years, so think beyond courses and extracurricular activities. An example has been provided.

SPECIFIC COLLEGE DETAIL	STORY OF HOW YOU CONNECT WITH THAT SPECIFIC DETAIL
Example: *Swarthmore College*	
Swarthmore's Music department offers an independent study during junior year.	No college offers a course in pop tune music forms. I showed a hook to a producer in Cleveland and after he heard it he said: "Where is the rest of the song?" In my junior year at Swarthmore I will add form to my hook.

SPECIFIC COLLEGE DETAIL	STORY OF HOW YOU CONNECT WITH THAT SPECIFIC DETAIL
College 1:	

SPECIFIC COLLEGE DETAIL	STORY OF HOW YOU CONNECT WITH THAT SPECIFIC DETAIL
College 2:	

SPECIFIC COLLEGE DETAIL	STORY OF HOW YOU CONNECT WITH THAT SPECIFIC DETAIL
College 3:	

As you research different colleges and build the list of schools where you plan to apply, look for colleges that nurture all three aspects of your future: your passions, your talents, and how you will support yourself as an independent adult. Whatever you are looking for in college, you can find it. Maybe you are not so good at tests because you prefer to work without time pressure? Then apply to colleges where grades are based on papers and group work (e.g., Sarah Lawrence College). Are you one of those people who need to do something for yourself to really learn it? Look for colleges where courses are interwoven with internships and work experience (e.g., Northeastern University). Do you love lots of academic subjects, but have no idea what you want to major in? Consider a college that allows you to create your own major such as New York University's Gallatin School of Individualized Study and University of Washington's Individualized Studies Department. Or perhaps you are looking for an interdisciplinary major such as Human Values? Or maybe you are looking for a school of a particular size? In order to find colleges that are a great fit for you, it helps to take the time to figure out what it is that you are looking for.

Outlier Advice About Standardized Tests

You don't need me to tell you that a lot of attention is paid to standardized tests in most high schools! Some students get sucked up into a frenzy to get higher and higher test scores. Super scoring (taking a composite score of your best scores from each section) is a bit like super sizing—it is more than you need, and just not good for you. It is fine to study for the SAT or ACT, and there are free test prep services in many local communities and online. The best test prep programs teach skills that help you manage other types of tests in high school and college. But a few more points on a standardized test will not differentiate you from fellow students in a competitive admissions climate.

Here are a few facts to help you understand your standardized test options and make your own decision:

> There are more than 800 colleges in the United States that do not require standardized test scores for admissions. See the list at www.fairtest.org/university/optional.
> The ACT covers a variety of subjects that you study in school, including basic science; the test is straightforward and fast-paced, and the Writing section is optional (if you take the ACT, include the Writing section).
> The SAT has fewer questions and layers in critical thinking skills in addition to content knowledge; there is a penalty for wrong answers, so more strategy enters into SAT success.
> In terms of college admissions, the ACT and SAT are completely interchangeable, so you need to take only one of them.

Standardized tests can help you review and consolidate what you have learned in high school and build valuable study and test-taking skills that will benefit you in college, but your test scores do not indicate your worth or value, and they are only one piece of the "holistic," big picture approach that most colleges use when reviewing your application. Here are five steps you can take to prepare for the SAT or ACT as a piece of the college admissions picture:

1. **Take the PSAT and the Plus, if they are offered by your school.** If your school does not offer the PSAT or the Plus test (Plus is like the PSAT for the ACT), try a free online test to see if you are better suited for the SAT or ACT (www.kaptest.com/pdf_files/college/sat-act-practice-test.pdf).

2. **Choose either the SAT or the ACT.** Then focus on that one test. There are dozens of free online resources to help you decide which test is right for you. And there are zillions of resources—free and paid courses and coaching, in classrooms and online—to help you prep for one test or the other. The ACT and SAT have different strategies and different rhythms, so it's helpful if you can focus on just one of them.

3. **Whether you choose the SAT or ACT, take it only once or at the most twice.** Many students, parents, and schools get swept up in test score frenzy, and students take the tests over and over seeking higher and higher scores. This is expensive and in my opinion a poor use of your valuable time. Pick a date, preferably one that is not packed with a lot of other tests, and study toward that test date. For instance, March of your junior year is great because it is before AP exams. Make a study plan, block out the time in your schedule, and stick to your plan. A little bit of time each day is much better than cramming. (This is called "distributed learning," and it is an important study skill.) If your actual test score is considerably below the scores you earn on practice tests, figure out which types of questions are tripping you up, study those, and take the test one more time.

4. **Take SAT subject tests in subjects you have studied in school.** SAT subject tests cover college level work in high school courses. They are a great indicator of college readiness, and selective colleges often require that you have taken two or three of them. Take SAT subject tests as soon as possible after the course in which the material is taught (May or June). If possible, take something in math or science and something in humanities. It is often helpful to get a study guide, so when you are reviewing for the test, you can make sure you understand all of the topics that will be covered on the test, including ones that may not have been covered in your high school class.

Focus on Your Strengths

It is so much better in the college process to identify and develop your core strengths than to try to "fix" what you may consider your "weaknesses." Take the time to identify your natural talents and find stories that reveal those strengths to others—particularly your strengths of character. Perhaps there are things you believe you could be good at, but have not really tried. How might you explore whether you will be good at them? Figure out what that is, and take the time to do it. For instance, you love clothes, and have thought about being a fashion designer. Learn what skills it takes to be a fashion designer and where you can acquire them. What have you already done using skills related to the ones required for your chosen field? If you can show colleges those connections, you are also showing them why they should invest in you to pursue that work in the future.

The Bridge chart (Exercise 2) explored connections between your past and your future, and Exercise 5: What You Bring to the Game, both earlier in this chapter, suggests the overlap of your passions, strengths, and possible career directions. Now is the time to start sharing those ideas with colleges in a way that gets their attention and helps them believe in you and advocate for you.

The Three-Sentence Story

You will learn all about planning and mapping your essays in Chapter 8. Here is a quick three-question test you can use to see if what you are telling is a story:

1. Does it happen in the world or in your mind? Stories happen in the world.
2. Can you tell it in three sentences—beginning, middle, and end?
3. If you change any one of the sentences, or the order of the sentences, do you have a completely different story?

The three-sentence story is a tool you can use to wrestle inchoate ideas into a cohesive shape, almost like taking a blob of clay and making a smooth, round sphere before you do anything else. Prepping for an interview? Plan three-sentence stories to demonstrate each of the points you want to get across. Do you have late night lab report blues? Try a three-sentence story to report what happened in the experiment and the results. Need to organize a big research paper? Use the three-sentence story as a way to structure the argument.

Ready to take that leap off your comfortable stone? In the next exercise you will write about one of your most important activities from The Bridge.

Bring Activities to Life

In essays—and especially in interviews—you will be asked to talk about your most important work and extracurricular activities. To answer this type of question, pick one of the activities from The Bridge (Exercise 2). Tell a three-sentence story that shows you engaged in that activity. What does that activity show about your character and commitment? Describe a moment when you changed or grew or made a difference. Pick a moment that has a beginning, middle, and end, and write it below until you fill the page.

_____

_____

_____

_____

_____

_____

_____

_____

_____

_____

_____

_____

_____

_____

_____

_____

_____

_____

_____

Now you have a short essay about an activity that is important to you. You will revise this essay later, and you will explore short essays about other activities, once you have some more tools. You have begun to write your Story To College—the moments in your life when things changed—and you have started to explore your possible futures. Chapter 3: Transform Scripts to Stories teaches you how to get past the stories that everyone tells to those that are uniquely your own.

Further Reading

Nelson-Bolles, Richard. *What Color Is Your Parachute? A Practical Manual for Job-Hunters and Career-Changers*. 2013 ed., rev. ed. Berkeley: Ten Speed Press, 2013.

Rath, Tom. *Strengthsfinder 2.0*. New York: Gallup Press, 2007 and online at www.strengthsfinder .com/home.aspx.

CHAPTER 3

Transform Scripts to Stories

*Storytelling reveals meaning without ever
committing the error of defining it.*

—HANNAH ARENDT[1]

People often speak in scripts. And most students write college application essays that sound like scripts too. You can think of scripts as shorthand, ways you talk and write that are formulaic. Scripts have safe, rounded edges and attractive wrapping. They lack the bumps, bruises, and messiness of everyday life. Scripts are important because they help us understand the past and plan for the future. "I've always wanted to be a doctor," you might say, or "I'm a creative person." A college application essay written as a script ends with a big moral lesson, such as "That was the day I learned that all people are equal," almost like a fairy tale.

In the Moments Method we define "scripts" as clichés, generalizations, and things that anyone can say—all writing that applies to everyone but says nothing specific about anyone in particular. We tend to hang on to our scripts and use them over and over without thinking. There are three ways that scripts suck the life out of college application essays:

1. **Scripts are general.** Scripts apply to everyone, in a general sort of way, but they say nothing specific about *you*.
2. **Scripts are predictable.** Everyone uses them. If you have just a few seconds to capture someone's attention, the last thing you want to be is predictable.
3. **Scripts can be off-putting.** They are true in a general way but are not true about real people. They are almost too good to be true.

REFRESH

My Alter Ego

If you were a character from a book, movie, television show, or video game, who would you be? Write down the first character that comes to mind:

Then describe all the things you have in common with that character—they always wear flannel shirts, you were both born in Oklahoma, you both love orange lollipops . . . just as many details as you can think of that make you like your character. Set a timer and keep your pen moving or your fingers typing for three minutes or more.

The Trouble with Scripts

The most successful college essays are *never* based on scripts. Why not?

Scripts bounce around on the surface, but they do not connect. We are attracted to people who are more nuanced and complicated; we want to know more about them. This is how our brains work, and why we often make irrational decisions based on a swirl of emotion and memory. To write successful personal essays, you want to tap into admissions readers' memories and emotions. To do that you want to open up your scripts, let their perfectly safe borders soften a bit, and explore some of your ambiguities and challenges. In this chapter, you will take the scripts you say about yourself, clichés you think you are supposed to say, and stories that other people say about you, and begin to find stories that are specific and unique to you.

While you are letting go of what works in other contexts but not for your college essays, remember that personal essays work in a completely different way from the critical essays you are taught to write in English class. So forget about stating a general introduction, showing examples, and then repeating how great you are in the conclusion.

Critical Essays vs. Personal Essays

What is the difference between a personal essay and a critical essay? A critical essay—the kind you write in English class—is structured like an argument. In high school many students are taught to write critical essays in a five-paragraph format: introduction, three supporting paragraphs, and a conclusion. You tell people what you are going to argue, you support your argument with evidence, and then you summarize it.

WHAT MAKES A GREAT CRITICAL ESSAY?
Argumentative structure
Successful when facts support ideas
Logical, unemotional
Ends complete

There is nothing wrong with critical essays; in fact, most of the work you do in college—and a great deal of professional writing—will be built on this foundation. But the model of a critical essay is the opposite of what works in a college application essay—which is also called a "personal statement" or "personal essay" because it is about you as a person.

A personal essay moves with the energy of a story. Like great fiction, a successful personal essay draws you in from the very first sentence, and sticks with you long after you've put it down. Years later you may remember a striking detail or an unusual turn of phrase. It leaves you asking questions about the characters, the world, and the author's point of view.

WHAT WORKS IN A PERSONAL ESSAY?

Narrative structure

Successful when details and description draw reader in

Emotionally moving

Ends with reader wanting more

So, if you want to connect with your reader, you need to access a different skill set than the one you use for English class. You need to write from your right brain, the part that fosters empathy, compassion, and community in others. It turns out that storytelling is one of the best and most enduring ways to access all of that right brain connectivity.[2]

Want to read great personal narratives by famous authors? You can access them at our website at www.storytocollege.com/writeoutloud.

Personal Essays

Personal essays are most powerful when readers are drawn into your world. Readers see that world from your unique perspective, and they experience the moments that have shaped you as a human being. Scripts are too perfect and too polished to connect with people, especially when you have a very short time to make an impression. The first time a college admissions officer reads your essay will be very quick, just a few minutes. At first the reader will be filling in the picture drawn by other parts of your application: grades, test scores, work and extracurricular activities, and teachers' recommendations. You want to capture your reader's attention, draw that reader into your world, and give him or her a sense of who you are as a person. When you introduce the reader to the real human being who has accomplished all the other things in your application, you show why your application—and you—should be given more attention.

Before we start transforming your scripts to stories, I want to dispel a few common misconceptions about college application essays. Most high school students start out thinking that a great college essay is a script ("What essay do colleges want?" "Which personal statement will get me into College X?"). That approach almost never works. College admission officers read the essays *to get to know about you as a person*, so you need to start with who you are, not what colleges want.

Many students think that college essays should be about their achievements, their superhuman moments: how you got the best grade in your Calculus class or, after hard work, won the lead in the school play. But your achievements are included in other parts of the application. Essays are your chance to add a completely different perspective to your application. They are called personal essays because they show who you are as a person. Achievements are great, and *Write Out Loud* teaches you how to talk about your achievements in ways that bring them to life, revealing your character and personality. In general, achievements that show up somewhere else on your college application do not form the heart of great admissions essays.

Another misconception about college essays is that they need to be about lavish trips and fancy experiences. In fact, the most powerful essays often portray simple human moments to which many people can relate because they have experienced something similar. Great essays can be built around almost every moment of your life, including everyday experiences like cooking, cleaning, and conversation. My family dinner will be different from yours, but your family dinner story engages me by reminding me of my own.

A successful college application essay takes a moment to which others can relate and shows it from your unique point of view. Here is an example. Many people can say, "I'm passionate about the environment," or "I'm President of the Environment Club at my school," or "I joined the Environmental Club with my best friend and stayed after she left." Do any of these statements excite you and make you say, "Yes, I want to know more about this person"? Probably not! Scripts fall flat because they are predictable and boring. Your job in college essays is to connect with the reader. To make that connection you need to draw the reader into your specific way of seeing and doing things. You need to be a bit vulnerable—not by revealing moments of danger (though such moments can be shaped into great essays), but by shaping your moments of growth and change so they are palpable for others.

You bring your experience to life for your reader, again and again, by replacing generic scripts with specific stories that only you can tell. For instance, let's go back to our environmentalist. What is your experience of reading this version of her essay: "I worked with 15 eighth graders. We planned and planted a garden in Orange where an old hat factory was torn down. Three months later it's an overgrown jungle of purple, yellow, and green." There's a lot going on in those three sentences. I suspect that you became curious about the story because of the specific details (the 15 eighth graders, the hat factory, the "jungle" of colors) and the person who tells this story. There's also the quirky—and technically not grammatical—shifting of tenses from the past "planned and planted" to "it's" (short for "it is") that creates immediacy. In just three sentences, whether or not you care about the environment, you get a clear picture of what she did to make a difference in her local community. Her quirky story draws you in and makes you want to know more about her.

Something amazing happens between people when they tell stories. Storytelling triggers a complex web of brain activity that links human beings to one another. Community is built on storytelling—not conventional scripts, but unique stories told from your distinct point of view. When you tell your story, your brain experiences a combination of memories, emotions, and actions. And when other people listen to your story—whether you are telling it out loud or in writing—their brains experience the same combination of memory, emotion, and action, almost as if your story is happening to them. With storytelling you quite literally re-create your experience for another person. It's human nature; it's in our DNA; it works every time.[3]

Identifying Scripts

You don't have to be a neuroscientist or a professional writer to complete powerful college application essays. Every person has unique stories to tell from his or her own experience. You begin the process by turning the safe, superficial scripts you usually tell into more specific and nuanced stories. In this chapter, you will learn to recognize the scripts that you tend to tell about yourself, almost as if you are talking on autopilot. There are many kinds of scripts, and we use them all the time. Scripts can be stories other people tell about you: "He's my best friend" or "He's the captain of the baseball team." They are the general parts of life. Our brain tends to shut down when we hear scripts because we hear them over and over, and they are predictable. They capture many people's hopes and dreams, but they are not actually true, or not true in a specific way, about anyone.

Scripts are like armor. Scripts keep you safe and secure. However, like armor, scripts also keep others at a distance. In contrast, the best application essays reveal you with your armor down, when you are talking about your own experience in your own voice, as you would to a trusted friend. Some people think that college essays need to be intensely emotional—this is another misconception that is definitely not true. Essays that are too emotional can be as off-putting as essays that are flat and unemotional. Great essays are authentic, based on the details of your experience, the things that actual people say and do in everyday life. But they should not be too raw either.

This chapter teaches you how you can put your armor down a bit and let other people get to know you. Don't worry; you'll still be safe. Being the master of your own stories enables you to be both vulnerable and secure. You choose which stories you tell about yourself and to whom. But first, to begin putting down that armor, you need to recognize how often you (and most people) speak in scripts.

Here are some scripts you may recognize:

I've wanted to be pre-med since . . .
My mother says I'm . . .
I'm a first-generation college student . . .
I'm Black (or Jewish or Latina or Korean or mixed race) . . .
That was the day I learned . . .
I'm a leader . . .

Families often use scripts to place people in relation to one another and their core beliefs: "He's the prodigal son" or "She's my creative daughter" or "My family believes in the importance of education." Once you recognize them as scripts, you can start turning your own and other people's general ideas into stories that connect you powerfully with other people—in college admission essays, job interviews, and every aspect of life.

There are a variety of scripts we use without thinking; they are like crutches we lean on to get us through confusing and complicated moments:

> **What are the scripts that other people tell about you?** Are they true? Are there other parts of your story you wish people knew, but you do not share with them? My friend Donnica sometimes asks, a bit disarmingly, "What is the most important thing I don't already know about you?" What are the most important things that most people don't know about you?

> **What scripts do you use that are things lots of people can say, or that you think you are supposed to say?** "I want to be a doctor." "I have been in the same relationship for all of high school." "I am a great friend."
> **Which scripts do you use that are superficial and safe, and not true outside of fairy tales?** "In my family everyone gets along." "I grew up with small town values." "I never lie."

Scripts are static, fixed, and generally not very interesting because they do not reveal who you are as an individual. The next exercise helps you to identify your own and others' scripts.

EXERCISE 1

What Are Your Scripts?

What are the scripts your family tells about you?

1. _____

2. _____

3. _____

What are the scripts your friends tell about you?

1. _____

2. _____

3. _____

Pause right there for a second—if these are different, that's an interesting place to start paying attention.

What are the scripts you tell about yourself?

1. _____

2. _____

3. _____

Do you tell different scripts to different people? That's interesting too; honor those complexities.

What scripts do you think will get you into college? Honestly!

1. _____

2. _____

3. _____

Now, here are two questions you may have thought about, or even talked about with some of your close friends. But I have asked these questions in hundreds of college admission interviews over the past 30 years, and this is where most high school seniors start to fidget. You cannot fake these answers:

What difference do you want to make in the world?

1. _____

2. _____

3. _____

What do you want people to say about you at your funeral?

1. _____

2. _____

3. _____

Those last two questions can be answered with scripts too! And you may not have scripts—let alone stories—about your purpose in life. What if you could find that sense of purpose and make it palpable to others? That's what you will learn next, and it will give you a much greater chance of connecting with people. Once you connect with them, they will want to know more about you. And if they want to know more about you, they start thinking about you and imagining how you will make a difference in their community and they are much more likely to admit you to their college.

Transforming your scripts into stories is much bigger than just getting into college; it takes you from a predictable "anyone" to a living, breathing "someone," to paraphrase Emily Dickinson.[4] In the last exercise you identified your scripts, the hackneyed and predictable things you say about yourself, and others say about you, again and again. What, in contrast, is a story? And what does it mean to transform your scripts into stories?

Creating Stories

A story is based in actions, events that take place between specific people at a specific place and time. Stories can be quite simple. For instance, look at this three-sentence story: "I took a walk in the woods behind my house. I found a bird that had fallen out of its nest. I nursed it back to health." This is how you can use three-sentence stories to check if you have a story:

> Each of the three sentences is based in action.
> If you change any one of the actions, or the order of the actions, the story changes fundamentally.

Whenever you change the actions, or the order of the actions, the story produces a different emotional response in the reader. Here's how it works.

Let's say my script is "I care about animals." See what happens to that script as I change each of the sentences in my story (the changed sentences are in italics):

> "*I was crossing Pugh Street on the way to school.* I found a bird that had fallen out of its nest. I nursed it back to health."
> "I took a walk in the woods behind my house. *I found a deer that had been shot and left for dead.* I nursed it back to health."
> "I took a walk in the woods behind my house. I found a bird that had fallen out of its nest. *I ran back to the house and wrote a poem.*"

When I change any one of the three sentences, my story is based in a completely different set of actions and produces a completely different emotional response in the reader.

Every story you tell reveals a trove of information about your view of the world, your choices, and your priorities. Small changes make a big difference. In different versions of this three-sentence story, the author is a budding country veterinarian, an urban environmentalist, or a poet. In one version she takes on a small project, and in the other a project that is almost too big to be real. (I grew up in deer hunting country, by the way, and I did once find a deer wounded by a hunter. I did not eat venison again for 22 years.) In two versions of the story the speaker takes action, and in one she pauses to reflect. Stories bring your passions and beliefs to life by showing what you have done about them. The person who nurses a bird or deer back to health does not have to say, "I care about animals." We figure that out for ourselves from every version of that three-sentence story. (Extra credit here if you noticed "I nursed it back to health" is also a script.) We also see that the person who tells that story is a fixer, a healer, and someone with compassion.

Each story you tell connects with the reader in a wide variety of ways and helps that reader understand you and relate to you. Different readers will connect with different details. The reader can't help but be attracted to you through your stories. Even when we disagree with a person's ideas, our brains love stories, and we are emotionally drawn to the people who tell them.[5] Since each person remembers events differently, even people who participated in the same event will remember different details and tell vastly different stories. Your way of remembering and telling your stories is completely your own.[6] When you transform scripts to stories, you capture the reader's attention and draw that person into your unique way of experiencing the world. Every story reveals information about your view of the world, your choices, and your priorities. Stories bring your passions and beliefs to life by showing what you have done about them.

Stories are based in actions. Stories are fluid. Stories have multiple perspectives. While scripts are static and safe, stories are more open and available. If we tend to tell scripts to inoculate and protect ourselves, we tell stories to connect with others. Now here's something to keep in mind: a story can always turn back into a script. Tell it often enough, exactly the same way, and the edges begin to harden. Think about the stories your grandparents tell—your grandmother may be a great storyteller, but what she says is fixed. Her stories probably change very little from Thanksgiving to Christmas or from year to year. When you are a grandparent you can tell those same stories, again and again, but for now your job is to *reveal who you are*, and you cannot do that by recycling other people's stories. Sorry, it will not work. In order to connect with another person—whether in a college application, a job interview, or a first date—scripts fall flat. Still don't believe me? At the end of the chapter, there's a little test. Here are some exercises to warm you up first.

Some of our most influential stories are our "tales of the tribe," the stories our families tell again and again (one of mine is about my grandfather walking to the docks in Philadelphia when he first came to the United States as a teenager, buying fish and selling it on the streets). We all have these stories, and they form an important part of our own personal stories. In Chapter 10: Explore Perspectives, you will return to these stories and learn how to write essays about people and things that have influenced you. What are your family's foundational stories?

EXERCISE 2

Family Stories

List at least eight stories that your family tells about itself.

1. _____

2. _____

3. _____

4. _____

5. _____

6. _____

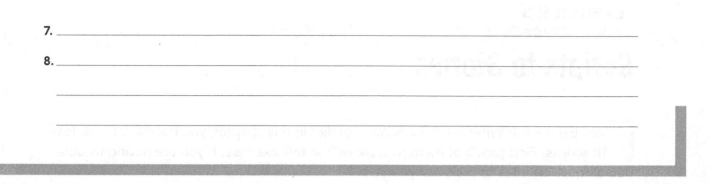

7. _____

8. _____

_____

_____

At this point students sometimes say, "But I can't find any stories of my own. My parents' stories are more interesting. I haven't done anything important enough." It may take some sifting and sorting to get to the stories that reveal who you are as a human being, so try to be patient. I promise you have lots of great stories—everyone does; almost any moment of your life can be shaped into a story—but your stories may not be where you are looking for them at first. So let's start turning your habitual scripts into more specific stories. The next exercise starts to open up the scripts you and others tell to find meatier, more engaging stuff. First let's explore what I mean by scripts versus stories and give some examples of each.

A script is a general statement that is not specific to anyone in particular (e.g., "My family believes in the value of education"). There are three types of scripts:

> **Interpretations** are judgments about what you are describing (e.g., "It was the worst day of my life").
> **Internal dialogue** is what you are thinking (e.g., "I was thinking about my father").
> **Emotion** is your feelings explicitly stated (e.g., "I felt sad").

A story, in contrast, is something that happened to you told from your perspective (e.g., "I went to the 7-11 on the corner of Amsterdam and 125th to buy chocolate milk"). There are three things that characterize stories:

> **Actions** are events that take place in the world (e.g., "My father drove home from New York").
> **External dialogue** is the exact words that people say (e.g., "My sister said, 'Get your nose out of your schoolwork, Carol. Daddy is coming home today'").
> **Description** includes sensory details and other specific information (e.g., "He had a purple rash on his face, his stomach was bloated, and his breath smelled rancid").

Scripts to Stories

From Exercise 1: What Are Your Scripts, earlier in this chapter, you have a list of at least 18 scripts. First pick 3 of them to work with in this exercise. If you are having trouble deciding which ones to pick, ask yourself:

> Which of my scripts feels most important or urgent to me right now?
> Which of my scripts is the most important thing I want colleges to know about me? You can also find this one—or other ideas—on your Bridge chart (Chapter 2).
> Which one of my scripts reveals something about me as a member of a college community?

Pick the 3 that are most urgent and most important and that reveal what you bring to a college community, and copy them below. In the next set of exercises, you are going to work with each of these scripts to find a variety of stories you can use to unpack them and make them your own in college admission essays.

1. _____

2. _____

3. _____

For each of those three scripts, you are going to say which kind of script it is (interpretation, emotion, or internal dialogue) and write down 10 stories that reveal something specific about you underneath the script. For example, perhaps your script about yourself is "I've wanted to be a doctor since fourth grade," and your family's script about you is "He loves kids; he'll be a great pediatrician." You do want to be a doctor, but maybe not a pediatrician, and you wish your family didn't talk about it so much because it feels very constraining to have everything all decided already. That is a great script to explore further in the next exercise, delving into your journey from fourth grade to today, and focusing on the moments along the way that formed your ideas about yourself and your actions as a future doctor.

Experiences to Stories

Script 1

Type of script (interpretation, emotion, or inner dialogue) _____

10 STORIES

1. _____
2. _____
3. _____
4. _____
5. _____
6. _____
7. _____
8. _____
9. _____
10. _____

Script 2

Type of script (interpretation, emotion, or inner dialogue) _____

10 STORIES

1. _____
2. _____
3. _____
4. _____
5. _____
6. _____

7. _____

8. _____

9. _____

10. _____

Script 3 _____

Type of script (interpretation, emotion, or inner dialogue) _____

10 STORIES

1. _____

2. _____

3. _____

4. _____

5. _____

6. _____

7. _____

8. _____

9. _____

10. _____

This exercise may take some time. It may help to carry *Write Out Loud* around with you for a few days, so you give yourself time to get past the obvious answers and make it the whole way to 10 moments for each script. Why? Because the first things you come up with are likely to be things that are obvious. They may even be more scripts! To find stories that will surprise and engage both you and the person who reads your essay, you need to go past the obvious.

It is also possible that you will come up with stories that contradict the scripts. Write those down too! For instance you are an honest person, but there was that time—maybe back in second grade—when you stole your best friend's pencil case. You threw it in the garbage a couple days later, and never told anyone. You probably don't want to use that story by itself in a college application essay. But perhaps there was a moment in tenth grade when you were silent and secretive about something more complicated, and that memory came back to you. That's the beginning of an interesting story! You will figure out which stories you want to tell in your personal essays and supplements to each college. For now just get your stories out on paper. You can decide what you want to do with them later. The process begins by opening up your usual scripts and finding fresh stories, by remembering the experiences and moments that have shaped you into who you are today.

At the end of Exercise 4: Experiences to Stories, you should have 30 (or more) possible essay topics. This is the beginning of your personal arsenal of stories, your Story Portfolio.

EXERCISE 5

Story Portfolio

Make a list of all the stories you have come up with so far that reveal things that are important for colleges to know about you.

_____

_____

_____

_____

_____

_____

_____

_____

_____

_____

_____

_____

_____

_____

_____

_____

Over the next nine chapters you will refine your Story Portfolio, add to it, and draw from it to answer different types of questions that are asked in personal statements and supplement essays for each college. The Story Portfolio is yours to build and share with others. You decide which stories you want to tell in your college applications, and which ones you prefer to keep to yourself. In Chapter 4: Choose a Moment you will start working with one of your many stories. But first some more exploration of specific colleges, an exercise to tie the work of this chapter together, and that test I promised you earlier!

Most stories students tell about colleges in their applications are very predictable scripts, such as "I walked onto the Haverford campus and knew it was the place for me." You should apply to colleges that are a great fit for you. This exercise helps you look at different colleges and imagine yourself at each of them, in a way that is based in your life story moving forward.

Connecting with College Courses

Pick three colleges you are interested in applying to. For each one, research online and pick three courses you might take. List them in the following chart. Then for each one write a three-sentence story that connects the work you are doing now with what you might study in college and how that may influence your future.

Example: *Boston College*

Major: *Sociology*

Course 1: *Sociology of Gender*

Course 2: *Race and Gender in the US*

Course 3: *Seminar: Race and Gender in US Social Movements*

In AP US History I researched the relationship between the movements for race and gender equality. The junior seminar on Race and Gender in US Social Movements will allow me to extend my research on race in the women's suffrage movement. This will inform my volunteer work with young single mothers who are completing high school.

College 1:

Major: _____

Course 1: _____

Course 2: _____

Course 3: _____

_____

_____

_____

_____

_____

College 2:

Major: _____

Course 1: _____

Course 2: _____

Course 3: _____

_____

_____

_____

_____

College 3:

Major: _____

Course 1: _____

Course 2: _____

Course 3: _____

_____

_____

_____

_____

_____

You will connect most powerfully with the colleges where you have the strongest fit. That is why we have you start thinking about specific colleges as if you were a student there and exploring very specific details, including courses, activities, internships, and different career paths. College application essays are a process, back and forth between who you are today, what you want to do in the future, and which colleges can help you make the most powerful connections between your past and your future.

Sometimes at this point students say, "I just want to get my essays DONE! How do I decide which are the best topics for my college essays?" The next chapter helps you identify the stories that are most important for you to tell in your college application essays.

Scripts vs. Stories in Action

Here's the test I promised you! I have shown you how stories work and suggested why they are better than scripts (or facts) in connecting with other people, especially people you want to remember you and take positive action on your behalf. For the next 24 hours, your test is to observe how people talk. Just observe. Who speaks in scripts? Who speaks in stories? Which people are you attracted to? Which ones capture your attention? Which ones do you remember longer? Write your observations about how scripts and stories affect you here. If you are practicing *Write Out Loud* with a group of friends, discuss what you observed with them!

_____

_____

_____

_____

_____

_____

_____

_____

_____

_____

_____

_____

_____

_____

_____

_____

Remember that for any script there are an infinite number of potential stories. The more you practice the Moments Method the more you will connect with people, powerfully and authentically in every part of your life. So whenever you find yourself reverting to scripts, do a quick Refresh—let go of your doubts—choose a moment and tell a story instead. Chapter 4: Choose a Moment teaches you how to unleash the power of storytelling by focusing on specific defining moments.

Further Reading

Guber, Peter. _Tell to Win: Connect, Persuade, and Triumph with the Hidden Power of Story_. New York: Crown Business, 2011.

Light, Richard. _Making the Most of College: Students Speak Their Minds_. Cambridge, Mass: Harvard University Press, 2001.

Pink, Daniel H. _A Whole New Mind: Why Right-Brainers Will Rule the Future_. New York: Riverhead Books, 2006.

CHAPTER 4

Choose a Moment

> When, years later, she'd look back at this moment of change, look at it
> clinically . . . she would see that her transformation actually took place
> over many months. However, it was only as she was falling out of the sky
> over the Bab al-Mandab that she understood that change had come.
>
> **—ABRAHAM VERGHESE, *CUTTING FOR STONE*[1]**

In every experience that defines you, there is a moment of change, a moment after which the world looks different. You say and do things differently. You make different choices. Others may not notice at first, but your perspective has changed. You have changed. You know it, and feel it. There is a clear before and after. How do you bring these moments to life so other people can experience what has changed for you? In this chapter you will learn to find those moments and explore them. You will explore your own Defining Moments to find the details that make those moments accessible to others.

The Moments Method

Students often try to pack too much into each essay. They will write essays that start like this: "From being the stage manager I learned how to work with other people and how all the parts of a play are put together. The director said he could really count on me to take care of things." Did you notice three scripts in those two sentences? And then the person provides a laundry list of all the things he or she did as stage manager. The experience of being the stage manager suggests that this person is probably a great bet for management of a campus organization! Sound like you? How can you make your leadership experience come to life for your reader?

REFRESH

Yesterday

What did you do yesterday? Write down everything you can remember, including as much sensory detail as possible. No scripts! What did you do? What did people say? What else did you hear? What did you smell and taste? What did your hands do and touch? Write everything you can think of and keep your pen moving or your fingers typing for three minutes or more.

Here's the secret: drawing me into one critical moment of that experience will show me much more than a laundry list of all the things you organized. Pick one detail for each essay, and relegate everything else to your résumé. Let's say as stage manager you were responsible for the program, the lighting, the props, the costumes, and makeup. What are the key stories in each of those areas, and what are the specific moments that make up those stories? A moment is a specific and contained instant in time when something changes. Most of the things we first call "moments" are actually stories comprised of many moments, so go in as close as you can to distinguish specific moments from a very generalized experience. Maybe the lighting was a week behind schedule, and you worked with the director and lighting team to rethink the lights, making them simpler but also more powerful. Maybe you delegated the program to someone who doesn't usually do graphic design, and you taught her how to use InDesign. Or maybe the person in charge of makeup got sick, and you had to convince the big, burly male lead, who is also the captain of the football team, to wear lipstick on stage. This chapter teaches you how to choose a specific moment and work with it, so that it reveals your character and personality to the reader.

Choose a Moment is the fourth and final tool to find your stories and the heart of the Moments Method: by drawing other people into your moments of growth and change you show them the world from your perspective, and you connect with them. Sharing the process that has shaped you into who you are today shows admissions readers what you are likely to do when you are tested in the future—on their college campuses and in the rest of your life. In this chapter you will organize the work you did in Chapter 2: The Bridge and Chapter 3: Transform Scripts to Stories. Choose one moment that reveals something important about your character—I call this a Defining Moment—and go back and explore that moment from various perspectives. In Part 2 and Part 3 you will work with a variety of different moments from your Story Portfolio and shape them into college application essay drafts.

While you are going back into your Defining Moments, you want to remember and write down everything you find there, as vividly and in as much detail as possible. The more you can remember, the more you will have to work with in your actual essays. Allow yourself to be curious about what is there. When you are digging around in one Defining Moment, you may remember others—just write down what you find in your Story Portfolio and you can explore those moments later.

The Moments Method is a process you can use again and again to identify the key moments from your own past and focus in closely to bring them to life for others. For instance, every one of my generation remembers the day that President Kennedy was shot. I was in kindergarten, and we were sent home from school early. When I got home everyone—10 people who worked for my parents in the advertising agency in the basement of our house—were all sitting on the coach in the living room, watching the news on our 20-inch black-and-white Zenith TV. Similarly, my children—who were 13, 11, and 7 on September 11, 2001, remember the angry crowds they saw cheering on television and the smell of burning oil. But that is all ancient history for you. Let's Refresh and go back to exploring your Defining Moments.

The next exercise gathers the work you did in the last two chapters and brings it together into what we will call your Life in Moments.

My Life in Moments

You will need The Bridge (Chapter 2) and your Story Portfolio (Chapter 3) to complete your Life in Moments. To complete the left side—What do I want colleges to know about me?—pull the most important elements from The Bridge. Include six to eight things, and at least one from each box in The Bridge.

Then, to complete the right side—My Life Story—review your Story Portfolio and list the major events of your life in chronological order. Include a few events from elementary school and middle school, but make at least half the list from high school or after leaving high school, and remember to include things you have done outside of school.

WHAT DO I WANT COLLEGES TO KNOW ABOUT ME?	MY LIFE STORY
I started a dance group at my school. My mother was a single mom and a huge influence. I want to study public health policy in college.	I was born. My brother was born a year later. When I was in third grade my grandmother died (she lived with us and was a dancer with Alvin Ailey until my mom was born). I started dancing after she died. In middle school my mother got sick, and I had to take care of her and my brother a lot. I was selected for a middle school pre-college program and applied to SEED for high school. I moved to the SEED school (this was really hard for me). Once a month my ninth-grade English teacher had us write poetry. I won a national poetry contest in tenth grade. Used the prize money to enroll in a summer dance program and started the Modern Dance Club at my school. The next summer I had an internship on Capitol Hill about public health policy.

WHAT DO I WANT COLLEGES TO KNOW ABOUT ME?	MY LIFE STORY

How to Choose a Moment

Choosing a moment is taking a specific moment out of a larger experience and exploring it from different angles, to identify how that moment was definitional for you. This is a bit like going to the gym and working one muscle group at a time. Some of your storytelling muscles may feel a bit awkward at first. But with time it will become more natural to use them, individually and together, and you will be able to use the power of your experience to connect with people in college applications and many other situations.

EOP, HEOP, and QuestBridge

There are a number of programs designed to make college accessible to students who would otherwise not be able to attend college.

> **The Education Opportunity Program** (EOP) provides full tuition for educationally disadvantaged students at state universities and community colleges around the United States.

> **The Higher Education Opportunity Program**, or HEOP, (http://heop.org/) is a New York State program that makes college available and affordable for economically disadvantaged students. HEOP offers tutoring and counseling to help with college adjustment. Students must have a household income of less than $40,000 for a family of four to qualify for HEOP. The program offers full tuition. Other states have similar programs; ask your guidance counselor for more information.

> **QuestBridge** (www.questbridge.org/) matches highly qualified, underserved students with selective colleges. In order to qualify, students must have a stellar academic profile (most QuestBridge scholars are in the top 5 percent of their high school class) and a household income less than $60,000 for a family of four. The program provides full tuition for all four years of college. Students applying to QuestBridge rank their top 8 schools from a list of 33 participating institutions (including Columbia, Dartmouth, Haverford, Northwestern, Stanford, Wesleyan, and Yale), and QuestBridge sends the strongest applications they receive to their partner schools. The schools then offer admission to the students they want; those offers are binding. About 1,500 students are matched through QuestBridge each year.

Whenever you move from a broad and general experience to something that is uniquely your own and show how a specific moment changed you, or allowed you to do something in the world, you stimulate the centers for compassion and empathy in the reader's brain.[2] You are reaching out as one human being to another; the other person's memories wake up and that person feels a sense of community with you. The first step is to sift through your experiences to find your Defining Moments and fill them in with details from your own remembered experience. The next exercise—Choose a Moment—gives you practice doing that.

Choose a Moment

Go back to Exercise 1: My Life in Moments, earlier in this chapter, and ask yourself, "What is the most important thing I want colleges to know about me?" (from the left side of the chart) and write it here:

_____

_____

Then ask yourself, "Which of my stories reveals some aspect of how that came to be my most important thing?" (from the right side of the chart) and write that here:

_____

_____

Following the trajectory of the example in Exercise 1, the most important thing she wants people to know is that she is resilient and resourceful. She chooses the story about starting a dance program at her school to reveal how she keeps going when she runs into challenges. Don't worry about which moment you pick. Just pick one of your characteristics and one of your important moments.

Moving from an Experience to a Defining Moment

The next exercise opens up one of your important life events from an Experience to a Moment to a Defining Moment. You create a Defining Moment by taking it out of the ebb and flow of everyday experience and focusing on specific actions, words, and details to show the reader what you have learned and how you have changed.

Here's the path you will follow:

> An **Experience** is the first way we remember things, rather broad and almost factual. Example: "My younger sister was born when I was 13."
> A **Moment** is a part of that experience that you remember specifically. Example: "When my father brought my baby sister home from the hospital, my mother stayed in the hospital. She was still too weak to come home."
> Out of your many experiences and memories, a **Defining Moment** is one that has changed you or someone else in some way. Example: "My father said, 'It may be a few weeks before Mama is strong enough to come home. I'm going to need you to step up and take care of your baby sister.'"

You can use the power of memory to open up your general experiences into specific Defining Moments of learning, growth, or change, and to connect your story with your reader's memories, emotions, and compassion, forging a powerful human connection with them.

EXERCISE 3

Experience ⟶ Moments ⟶ Defining Moment

Starting with the story you chose in Exercise 2: Choose a Moment, you are going to expand the story from an experience to a series of moments and then a Defining Moment, like the following example:

Experience

I started my school's Modern Dance Club.

Moments

The principal signed the letter of approval for the club.
Jack, Charles, and Diana danced on stage with the rest of the group.
I choreographed a new dance.
We all danced my piece in the school's Winter Festival.

Defining Moment

I dedicated the dance to my grandmother, who had danced with Alvin Ailey but left dancing to raise my mom. When the dance was over, I asked all the moms and grandmas in the audience to come on stage and stand with us.

Experience

_____

_____

_____

Moments

_____

_____

_____

_____

_____

_____

_____

Defining Moment

_____

_____

_____

_____

_____

_____

_____

_____

_____

_____

_____

_____

_____

The two biggest mistakes most students make in their college application essays are

1. Staying too broad and general
2. Telling stories that happen in their heads

Remember moments are only definitional if something happens in the world. Your big insights—something you learn, but you do nothing differently—are not the best topics for personal essays. What you learn is important; your ideas inform who you are and what you choose to do. But to make your unique insights accessible to other people, you need to reveal something you did or made happen in the world.

Here are some questions to ask yourself or your friends to turn an idea or realization into a Defining Moment:

> How did I get to the moment?
> What happened before the moment?
> What was different after the moment?

The more you explore the details of your story and share those details with your reader, the more powerful your essay will be.

Four Types of Defining Moments

Another way to think about your Defining Moment is to ask yourself, "What type of moment is this?" Most Defining Moments fall into one of four buckets:

> **Change:** Significant moments make a change in you or in the world.
> **Achievement:** You overcome an obstacle to make something happen in your own or someone else's life.
> **Risk:** You do something that is challenging or uncomfortable.
> **Dilemma:** You are forced to make a hard choice.

To find additional material, a Defining Moment can be explored from each of these perspectives. Next is an exercise to explore your Defining Moment using each of the four frameworks to reveal more information about what you learned and how you changed.

Defining the Moment

Consider the Defining Moment that you have been working with in the past two exercises. First write down the Defining Moment here:

EXAMPLE: *I dedicated the dance to my grandmother, who had danced with Alvin Ailey but left dancing to raise my mom. When the dance was over, I asked all the moms and grandmas in the audience to come on stage and stand with us.*

_____

_____

_____

_____

Now consider your moment from each of the following perspectives. Include a few in each category.

Change

EXAMPLE: *This was the first time that anything other than music was included in the Winter Festival.*

_____

_____

_____

Achievement

EXAMPLE: *There was an article about our performance in the local paper,*
with a picture of the dancers and their mothers and grandmothers
on stage.

Risk

EXAMPLE: *I was worried that some of the older women wouldn't be able to*
walk up the stairs onto the stage.

Dilemma

EXAMPLE: *My mom didn't want me to tell her story, but I did anyway.*

You can use Exercise 4: Defining the Moment to explore your Defining Moment story for the tensions and complexities that make it more engaging for the reader. And you can use the next exercise—Expand the Moment—to break the moment down into its component parts.

Expand the Moment

To find and write down the details that will leave an indelible impression with your reader, ask yourself questions as if you are an observer or reporter on your own experience. Be as specific as you can about colors, sounds, textures, and the words that people actually say. Feel free to add as many of your own questions as you need to find the important details.

Who?

Who was there? Were any of the people more important than the others? What were their names?

_____

_____

_____

What?

What did they look like? What did they wear? What did they say? Was there anything unusual that I would have noticed if I were there?

_____

_____

_____

When?

What season was it? What time of day?

_____

_____

_____

Where?

What is the name of the neighborhood or street? Is it inside or outside? Is it a public or a private place?

_____

_____

_____

Why?

This question tends to bring up interpretations. Once you figure out the why, can you find story details that show the why without the word _because_?

_____

_____

_____

Be an Outsider

Looking at your own experience with an outsider's questions can help you find aspects of your stories that you usually overlook. Any time that you explore this observer perspective—almost like watching your life from the outside—you are developing your capacity for reflection, which is not only at the heart of great essays, but an attribute of college readiness and college success.[3]

Cultivating the perspective of an outsider (the observer or reporter) helps you to re-experience the moments that have been fundamental in shaping you. This stance also helps you share your stories with others. For most of this chapter you looked at one story in considerable depth and from a number of different angles. The next exercise—Three by Three Life Stories—is designed to reveal important stories that you may have overlooked until now.

Three by Three Life Stories

This exercise works in three rounds.

ROUND 1: Write your life story in three sentences.

1. _____

_____

2. _____

_____

3. _____

_____

ROUND 2: Write your life story in three sentences, using none of the details you used in Round 1.

1. _____

_____

2. _____

_____

_____

3. _____

_____

ROUND 3: Write your life story in three sentences, using none of the details you used in Round 1 or Round 2.

1. _____

_____

2. _____

_____

3. _____

_____

If this exercise helped you find other moments that have been definitional for you, feel free to add them to your Story Portfolio (Chapter 3) to shape in the following chapters. As you shape your stories into college application essays, you will remember other moments, other stories. Write down these memories when you remember them, so you can explore them further and weave them into your college applications and your life story in the present.

Further Reading

Cron, Lisa. *Wired for Story*. Berkeley, CA: Ten Speed Press, 2012.

Defining Moment stories from great authors (links are also available at www.storytocollege.com/writeoutloud):

Blow, Charles M. "My Very Own Captain America." *New York Times,* July 29, 2011. www.nytimes.com/2011/07/30/opinion/blow-my-very-own-captain-america.html.

Eliot, T.S. "Tradition and the Individual Talent." www.bartleby.com/200/sw4.html.

Hughes, Langston. "Salvation." www.courses.vcu.edu/ENG200-dwc/hughes.htm.

Huneker, James. "Coney Island at Night." http://grammar.about.com/od/classicessays/a/Coney-Island-At-Night-By-James-Huneker.htm.

Jeoung, May. "Welcomed with Open Arms in Mumbai." *New York Times*, July 5, 2012. www.nytimes.com/2012/07/08/fashion/forgoing-a-shortcut-on-the-path-to-happiness-modern-love-not-enough-to-give-modern-love.html?pagewanted=all&_r=0.

Morrison, Toni. "The Day and Its Splendid Parts." *New York Times*, March 27, 2008. http://artsbeat.blogs.nytimes.com/2008/03/27/the-day-and-its-splendid-parts/.

Neale Hurston, Zora. "How It Feels to Be Colored Me." http://grammar.about.com/od/60essays/a/theireyesessay.htm.

Quindlen, Anna. "Homeless." http://pers.dadeschools.net/prodev/homelesstext.htm.

Woolf, Virginia. "Old Mrs. Grey." http://s.spachman.tripod.com/Woolf/oldmrsgrey.htm.

PART 2

SHAPE

CHAPTER 5

Tell It Out Loud

*Courage is what it takes to stand up and speak; courage
is also what it takes to sit down and listen.*

—ATTRIBUTED TO WINSTON CHURCHILL[1]

From the work you completed in Part 1: Find, you now have a portfolio of stories based on your own life experience. Great work! These stories—plus others you will remember and others that occur in your life in the present—provide the foundation for dozens of powerful and successful college application essays. You also explored at least one of your stories in detail as a Defining Moment: a time when you learned or grew or made a difference in some lasting and fundamental way.

Bravo! Give yourself a pat on the back! Most students never do this work, and, as a result, their college application essays are bland and generic. Those students' essays sound like they were written by a College Essay Generator machine, rather than by living, breathing people. By doing this work, you have set yourself up to write stronger, more authentic, and more compelling personal essays on your college applications. You are also paving the road to leadership, since storytelling is associated with entrepreneurship and business success.[2] In the next four chapters you will learn, step-by-step, how to shape your personal stories into powerfully moving application essays. If you are applying to a dozen colleges, as many students do, you will need to complete many different essays of varying lengths. This section gives you the tools and practice to shape your personal stories into essays that respond to the specific questions different colleges ask on their applications and supplements.

REFRESH

Listening

Use this Refresh to explore listening. What do you want in your ideal audience? What kind of person do you like to talk to? Maybe there are other things that help you to listen—some people like silence; others like a bit of background music. Perhaps there is a special place. Take five minutes and write down, keeping your pen moving or your fingers typing, everything you associate with listening, including what it is like to experience the absence of listening.

What Is "Fit" Anyway?

One of the things admissions counselors talk about a lot is "fit." They are looking for students who are a good "fit" for their colleges. But what do they mean by "fit," and how will you know if you have found it?

> Does the college have the majors you are looking for? Start your research at the college's website. Does it have academic programs in the fields you think you want to study?

> Does the college have strong career services and counseling services?

> And what about financial aid? How likely are you to receive the aid you need at the schools you are applying to?

> What types of internships and study abroad programs does the college offer? Will your financial aid travel with you if you want to study abroad?

> And what about extracurricular activities? Does the college have the activities that are an important part of your life outside of the classroom? You can also talk to students who attend the college—either through live chat on the college's website or through a friend of a friend. Most college students love to talk about their colleges!

> You should take the Scattergrams in Naviance with a grain of salt—because they tell you very little about individuals—but numbers do provide a reality check. You can also find the average grades and test scores of admitted students on the college's website. It is fine to apply to a couple of reach schools, but the core of your list should be schools where you will be a strong student.

> Finally, what about the school's culture and social life and its location? If you are really not interested in fraternities and sororities, then it probably is a bad idea to fill your list with colleges where frats govern the social scene. And if you want to go to college in a major city, then small-town schools are probably not a good fit.

There are many aspects of college, and the process of researching and visiting colleges provides a great chance to think about your future and talk about it with people who have different perspectives on college and on you: your parents, teachers, friends who are in college or have graduated from college. Even neighbors and local business people have useful insights about college, based on their own college experiences and everything they have done since. All these conversations will help you figure out, bit by bit, what types of colleges make the most sense for you.

Your Experiences and Moments Shape You

In Part 1 you looked into your life, almost as an archaeologist would, to find both your transformational experiences and your important everyday moments. Then you went deeper, exploring how those experiences and moments shaped you, and you connected your personal growth and learning with the difference you have been able to make in the world and the lives of people around you. Part 1 was all about you! Most high school students don't take the time to explore who they are and what difference they want to make in the world. They are so busy doing what they think other people want, or what they think they need to do to get into college, that they shortchange the process. Part 1 was a deep dive into your past and present, with tools to help you pay attention to the world around you, and to connect your past experiences with your future plans. The next four chapters teach you tools to take the experiences and moments you found in Part 1 and shape them in conversation and in writing.

Sometimes your life changes in tiny, almost imperceptible ways—you start picking up garbage around your school, let's say, or you decide to make fewer promises and stick to all of them, or you take up knitting on a whim. The idea in your college application essays is to make those moments of growth and change palpable, and to draw connections between the things that are important to you, what people count on you for, and where you are going and what you want to do in college and in life.

College Application Essays Are Like Conversations

It helps to think of each college application essay as a conversation. College admissions officers are reading your essays to get to know you. They are curious about what you will bring to their campuses and how you will make a difference. Shaping your stories is about connecting with an audience—in this case with college admissions officers at each of the colleges to which you are applying. In this chapter you will tell one of your Defining Moment stories to a friend. Telling your story out loud starts the process of shaping your experience into an essay that admissions readers will remember long after they have closed your folder and moved onto the next one. Then in Chapter 6: Write It Out, you will transcribe the story you told out loud and begin to shape it into an essay, maintaining the feeling and intimacy of a friendly conversation. Finally, in Chapter 7: Focus Out and Chapter 8: Map It, you will take your essay draft and work to make it both more vivid and more cohesive.

College admissions essays are like conversations in another way: they are written with a specific audience in mind. If I am talking to your parents, I will tell my story one way: "My guidance counselor said, 'Carol, no one from our high school has gotten into Yale for nine years. You will not be the next one.'" To students I will tell it another way: "The day before my father died, he said, 'Carol, you can go anywhere to college. Girls can go to any college they want now. You should look at Yale.'" It's not that the facts of my story change (college essays have to be the truth), but my emphasis changes. If I want to connect with each group, and I want them to understand me in a way that is meaningful, I have to speak specifically to them.

How Are Admissions Officers Reading Your Essays?

In June 2012 the University of Rochester invited me to speak at an annual meeting of 48 admissions officers from selective colleges and universities in New York State, including

Cornell, Hamilton, Union, and Syracuse. The topic was application essays, and the discussion was heated. Over the past decade, as the number of applications has increased dramatically each year, the essay has become more important relative to other factors. Most admissions officers read the essay either first or last, and they agreed that they read the essay to put other parts of the application "in a broader perspective." While the essay has become more important, students' essays have not improved. They have become more safe and predictable, the participants said, less valuable in distinguishing one student from another in the admissions process.[3] And while the essay is more important, the increased volume of applicants who all have strong grades and test scores means that admissions officers have less time to review individual essays.

In my survey of the 48 admissions officers before the meeting and in our discussion, they described what they are reading for—and what almost always turns them off![4]

> **The #1 thing they read for is strong writing.** Your application essays should be examples of your best work. The admissions officers' consensus was that most students don't spend enough time on their essays to make a "real impact."

> **They want to see a unique point of view.** They want to see the world as you see it, and they want to see what you have done. They pointed out that "unique point of view" is not the same as "expensive service trips" and "teen tours," which usually fail to impress.

> **Admissions officers crave "authenticity."** They say most students submit very "safe, generic essays that really don't help." The essay is the one place where you speak to admissions in your own voice, but "most students do not take advantage of this opportunity."

> **You don't want to sound "too crazy."** Your personal statement is like a first date with a stranger. What are the most important things you want them to learn about you right away? What things are better saved for later?

> **Essays are read in relation to other writing in your application.** If you have a very polished essay but low grades in English class or a poor SAT Writing score, colleges may assume that you did not write the essay yourself. Admissions officers reject up to 20 percent of applications because the essays seem to have been written by someone other than the applicant. On the other hand, if your essay is clean and simple and written in your own voice, no matter what your other scores, that is usually a plus.

> **Admissions officers often read your application essays when considering you for merit scholarships too.** "If I have a sense of who this person is, and how the programs we offer will make a difference in their life, I find myself nudging up the amount of aid we offer them," explained Tyler Socash from the University of Rochester, who organized the meeting.

> **Admissions officers use the essays and interview as a "reality check."** Even if you are unable to visit campus, set up a time to communicate directly when an admissions representative is in your area. And make sure to schedule those interviews for yourself—if your mother does the scheduling, you miss another chance to connect authentically.

> **Each college uses different guidelines to rank candidates.** Some recalculate your GPA so everyone is on the same scale; others look for criteria specific to their premier programs; and others seek students to lead important clubs and activities. These guidelines are different for every school but not mysterious. Take time to learn from their websites what colleges are looking for, and connect individually with each college to which you apply.

Most of all, admissions officers are reading for strong writing, a unique point of view, and an authentic voice. Your unique point of view lives and breathes in the details and structure of your story, which you will build in Part 2. In Part 3 you will learn how to edit your essays while maintaining the power of your spoken voice.

Telling Stories Out Loud

To make the most of Part 2, I recommend you find a friend and work together through these exercises. This can be someone who is not applying to college right now, or someone who is applying to different colleges from you—or at least not all of the same places. He or she should be someone you trust, who knows you, who will push you past where you usually stop, and who will tell you when your work is great, and also when it is not quite where it needs to be. Here is an exercise to warm up with your partner. Even if your partner is not applying to college, he or she can do all the storytelling exercises in this chapter—just for the fun of it.

EXERCISE 1

Memorable Meal Stories

You have two minutes to tell your partner a story about a memorable meal. Decide who will go first (who has the bigger feet is a good way to choose!), turn on a phone or other recording device, set a timer for two minutes, and the first person talks for two minutes. When the timer goes off, switch to another track on your recording device, reset the timer, and let the other person tell a memorable meal story for two minutes.

After you have both told your memorable meal stories, take a few minutes to talk about what it was like to listen to one another's stories. If your memorable meal story reveals something you want to work with later—perhaps in one of your application essays—go ahead and add it to your Story Portfolio in Chapter 3. In the next exercise you are going to tell one of your Defining Moment stories from Chapter 4 out loud. You will not need your notes or anything else—it is a story from your life, so you will remember it, and however you tell it is great. Just take a deep breath and jump in.

EXERCISE 2

Tell Your Story

This exercise really benefits from a live audience! Once again, you want to use either a cell phone or tape recorder as a recording device, and take turns timing and recording one another's stories. Before you start the recorder, do a quick 30-second Refresh to clear out any cobwebs of self-doubt or self-criticism that are hanging out in the corners of your college application attic. Then take a deep breath, and this time you have three minutes to tell a Defining Moment Story. Even if your partner is not completing the Write Out Loud process, he or she can still tell a story to you! Just explain what a Defining Moment is, give your partner about 10 minutes to find a story he or she wants to tell, and then all you have to do is listen!

Whenever you are stuck in your thoughts, ideas running amok with very little captured on paper, tell your story to another person and record the telling. Even telling your story to your phone or computer helps to get the juices flowing and activates your voice. Don't have a recorder? Ask a friend to take notes (by hand or on a laptop or smartphone) while you tell your story. And if you are somewhere alone, without a recorder, and want to get the essay process started with a new story, you can also write your story out by hand as if you are talking to another person, someone you really trust. By creating this sense of a personal conversation, as the space in which you shape your college application essays, you keep the essays warm and personal, as if you are in the room when the reader opens up your essay. The next exercise allows you to take this perspective on your own—or another person's—story.

If you are working through this book on your own, take some time to listen to stories told out loud on Story Corps (http://storycorps.org) or The Moth (http://themoth.org/stories). What is it like to listen to a story told out loud? What do you like about these stories? What do you remember a few days later? Where in your own life are those moments that will stick with people long after you have told them your story?

The Audience

What did you learn about this person from his or her story? Pretend you do not know the person already. What are your first impressions about this person from his or her story? List all the things you learned.

_____

_____

_____

_____

_____

_____

What was your experience of listening to the person's story? What happened when you listened to the story? Did the story trigger your memories? Which ones?

_____

_____

_____

_____

_____

What are you most likely to remember? Write down the details that you think will stick the longest.

_____

_____

_____

_____

_____

_____

Using Memorable Details

When you are shaping your spoken stories into written essays—as you will practice in the rest of *Write Out Loud*—keep this sense of the admissions reader listening to your story at the core of your writing and revision process. What is strongest in your spoken voice? Which details are most memorable? Expand those aspects of your story to answer whatever question you are asked—in writing or in conversation; in school, work, or the rest of life—and you will succeed in connecting with the other person. In the next exercise you will try this out by telling another story to answer the most important question of all, one you will be asked again and again: Why do you want to attend this college?

EXERCISE 4

Reading as Listening

Imagine you are reading college admissions essays. Read the following two essays, as if they have been written by two different students.

1. Community service will always be a big part of my life. Beyond the ordinary lectures in a classroom I hope to rigorously get involved with the clubs and activities offered at the University of Toronto. For example the Hip-Hop Marathon, where students raise more than one million dollars for world hunger by dancing 30 hours nonstop, is inspirational. One of the more creative organizations on campus that amused me is the Fair Wage Campaign, which advocates for service employees to be compensated fairly for their work. This in addition to the hundreds of other extracurricular activities intrigues me as I seek to get involved in community service, public speaking, and leadership.

2. I will be able to continue in the University of Toronto's tradition of community service by bringing 30-Hour Famine, an activity that I started at my high school. During 30-Hour Famine, I convinced 15 classmates to fast with me for 30 hours to raise awareness for hunger in East Africa. During our fast we stood in downtown Newark encouraging people with signs and shouts to honk their horns in support of our cause. In the 30-hour period I bonded with my fellow classmates for a cause that was greater than any one of us individually. The 30-Hour Famine fits perfectly at University of Toronto because it's similar to Hip-Hop Marathon. In the Hip-Hop Marathon, University of Toronto students raise more than one million dollars for world hunger by dancing 30 hours nonstop. Like 30-Hour Famine, the Hip-Hop Marathon seems like a fun way to get involved with fellow students and raise awareness for a cause.

What is the difference between the two essays? Which essay makes a more effective case for why the student should be admitted to the University of Toronto? How is that case made? If you could only admit one of them, which of these two students would you be more likely to admit to your college? Why?

_____

_____

_____

_____

_____

_____

Most people pick the second short essay. Why? The first example is full of scripts such as "Community service will always be a big part of my life" and "I hope to get involved" (a phrase that is used twice). In contrast, the second example depicts action and leadership: "I convinced 15 classmates to fast with me for 30 hours." Instead of listing lots of things (community service, public speaking, and leadership), the second essay focuses on community service and reveals the applicant's knowledge about the school's Hip-Hop Marathon while making a specific connection between Hip-Hop Marathon and the applicant's own experience starting 30-Hour Famine.

A great Why I Want to Attend Your College essay:

> Shows that you have researched the college to which you are applying
> Uses specific moments to make a connection between your life experience and your college aspirations

Now you are going to take what you learned from reading those two essays and use the power of your spoken voice to shape your first of many Why I Want to Attend Your College essays as if you were speaking out loud in an interview with an admissions officer.

Why Do You Want to Attend *This* College?

Why are you doing this now? This is probably the most important question of the whole application—Why do you want to attend this college? And most students put this question off until the last minute and then write things that are totally vague and predictable. True story: My nephew Josh was visiting Bucknell University. It was the first college he was visiting, and though my sister told him to do some research before they visited, he was busy with baseball and . . . you know how it goes. Josh and my sister arrived 10 minutes early at the Admissions Office, and they were shown into a big conference room. "Where are the other people?" Josh asked. Ten minutes later, a friendly man with a jacket and tie walked in and said, "Hi, this is your lucky day. I'm Bob Springall, Dean of Admissions, and you are the only one here this afternoon. Ask me anything you want about Bucknell." You never know when you are going to get your five minutes face-to-face with someone who can make a difference in your college future. So be ready! As my father always said, "Smart people learn from other people's mistakes."

Why I Want to Attend This College

Given your interests, values, and goals, explain why (X College/University) will help you grow (as a student and as a person) during your undergraduate years.

Key Points

An effective "Why College X" Essay:
1. Shows that you have researched the college to which you are applying
2. Uses specific moments to make a connection between your life experience and your college aspirations

Step 1: Select a College

What is your first choice college? _____

Step 2: Brainstorm

Write down at least five specific reasons why you want to attend this college (e.g., Swarthmore's Music Department offers an independent study during junior year).

_____

_____

_____

_____

_____

_____

Pick one college you would like to apply to, and fill in the following chart.

Why College X?

For each of the reasons you want to attend this college, write down three moments from your life that connect to this reason. Use extra paper if necessary.

REASON 1

MOMENTS

1.

2.

3.

REASON 2

MOMENTS

1.

2.

3.

REASON 3

MOMENTS

1.

2.

3.

REASON 4

MOMENTS

1.

2.

3.

REASON 5
MOMENTS
1.
2.
3.

Assess the moments you listed. Pick one that reveals an issue you may be involved

with in college: _____

Then—as if you have run into a college admissions officer in an elevator—tell that person why you want to attend his or her college. Tell the story of who you will be as a student there. If you have someone to talk to, tell it to that person; if not, just tell it to your phone or recorder. Stick to very specific details—what courses will you take, what programs will you pursue, which professor's work is interesting to you, what activities will you lead? Make connections with what you've already done. What difference will it make to have you as a part of that college community? Most Why I Want to Attend This College essays are 250 words or less, so there's no room for filler or fluff.

Strategy

The best college applications reveal your character; they show who you are as a human being. So for the main 650-world personal essay in the Writing section of the Common Application—or the long essay on another college application—you want to choose the story that reveals the most important thing about you, the thing that distinguishes you from students who are similar to you. You may be a scholarship student at a high school that gives very few scholarships. Or you may come from a family who arrived in the United States on the *Mayflower*, and so feel a little at odds with the American melting pot, salad bar utopian ideal. Most of us have things that we think about a lot but talk about rarely—important things we keep just beneath the surface in regular life. In your main personal essay, you want to bring one of those important but otherwise invisible things to the surface.

Quick Tips for Résumés

Many students find it helpful to have a simple, one-page résumé to bring to interviews and campus visits. Sometimes, if you get a bit nervous, you may forget some of the things you have done. A résumé helps keep it all right in front of you and gives the interviewer an overview and a place to start the conversation. Just put it on the table, or hand it to the interviewer at the start of the interview.

Here are some tips to remember when you are completing your résumé:

> **Put your most recent accomplishments at the top.** And make sure to keep your résumé up-to-date by adding new jobs, activities, and awards as they happen.
> **Prioritize the content.** Once you have it all in chronological order, put the part of the job with the most responsibility at the very top of its section.
> **Use verbs, verbs, verbs.** Use positive and active words to describe your skills and accomplishments.
> **Format cleanly.** People skim résumés more often than they read them, so make sure yours is easy to navigate. No fancy formatting or special characters are necessary, and resist the temptation to make your name super big to take up extra space!
> **Keep it under a page.** For most students, one page is plenty of room to include their high school job experience and related activities. Unless you won some sort of world prize or national championship in middle school, your résumé should start with high school. The one exception to this rule is if you have a long list of accomplishments in one specific field. For instance, if you have done four years of acting, directing, and producing in high school, you probably want to create a separate résumé for all of that experience to send to colleges with your arts portfolio.
> **Think "SMART."** Wherever possible, include **S**pecific, **M**easurable **A**ctions with **R**esults over **T**ime. For instance, "As sports editor I introduced 'Sports Puzzles,' a popular feature that was picked up by our town paper over the summer." Using your résumé to show what you did besides showing up will make a strong positive impact.
> **Proofread!** Use simple punctuation, and use it consistently. Have someone else proofread for spelling and consistency, if you possibly can.

Here are some websites for more information about how to build a successful high school résumé:

> eHow: How to Prepare a College Résumé: www.ehow.com/how_6932159_prepare -college-resume.html

> Top 12 Tips to Perfect Your College Resume: http://acceptedtocollege.com/blog/ application/20-tips-perfect-application-resume-1

> And here are some examples from Story To College Student Ambassadors: http://info.storytocollege.com/homerunresumes

In addition to Why I Want to Attend This College, you should use the shorter, supplemental essays required by colleges to add more detail to the story of what you bring to that particular college. The most successful supplement essays make specific connections between your experience and a specific college. So you need to complete really meaty research about each of the schools to which you are applying. And whenever you are completing an essay, I encourage you to answer the question using a story from your own experience that connects with the specific college you are talking to, just like a friendly conversation. Are you ready to write? The rest of *Write Out Loud* is all about writing!

Further Reading

Bohm, David, and Lee Nichol. *On Dialogue*. Routlege Classics ed. London: Routledge, 2004.

Steinberg, Jacques. *The Gatekeepers: Inside the Admissions Process of a Premier College*. New York: Penguin Books, 2003.

StoryCorps. StoryCorps describes itself as an independent nonprofit whose mission is to provide Americans of all backgrounds and beliefs with the opportunity to record, share, and preserve the stories of our lives. For more information see http://storycorps.org. To watch their animated shorts see http://storycorps.org/animation. Last modified January 2013.

The Moth. You can download podcasts of "true stories told out loud" on stage at The Moth at http:// themoth.org/stories.

CHAPTER 6

Write It Out

*Every secret of a writer's soul, every experience of his life,
every quality of his mind, is written large in his works.*

—VIRGINIA WOOLF[1]

Congratulations! You are halfway through *Write Out Loud*, and in this chapter you are going to start writing! The first step is to take one of your recorded stories (e.g., the one you told in Chapter 5: Tell It Out Loud) and write it out word for word.

Why Do We Tell Stories Out Loud and Then Transcribe?

Transcribing is the first step toward shaping your spoken story into a written essay. What do you gain by transcribing the stories you tell out loud?

> Transcribing allows you to assume the perspective of your audience.
> Transcribing enables you to experience your own spoken voice, its unique strengths and attributes.
> Transcribing teaches you how to be more intentional about your spoken voice, knowing how you sound to others.
> Transcribing is a means to assess and expand your public speaking skills.
> Transcribing prepares you to revise your essay, maintaining the power of your spoken voice in your writing.

REFRESH

What Is Writing?

What does writing mean to you? If you could not write what would you lose? What have people told you about writing? What have you been told about *your* writing? For five minutes, keeping your pen moving or your fingers typing, write down all of your ideas about writing.

Transcribing

Step 1

Listen to your whole story one time all the way through, uninterrupted. This allows you to experience the story as you told it, and to familiarize yourself with the way the story sounds when told out loud.

Step 2

What was your experience of listening to your own story in your own voice? Write down your thoughts here.

_____

_____

_____

_____

_____

Step 3

Type (or write out, if you prefer) what you hear, word for word, exactly as you told it. That means that your transcription should include every "like" or "um" and everything else exactly as you said it out loud.

_____

_____

_____

_____

_____

_____

_____

_____

_____

_____

Whenever you are stuck, feeling writer's block, or having trouble deciding how to edit your essays, you can always return to telling your stories out loud. Tell your story to a friend, or just walk around and tell it to yourself into your phone or recorder. Then transcribe it exactly as you said it so you have something on paper to work with. Telling your stories out loud keeps them close to your spoken voice. Whenever it feels like your writing is going in circles—go back to telling your story out loud. Ask yourself, "How would I say this, if I were speaking out loud?" Say it out loud and record your voice, and often that is enough to get your essay past where it has gotten stuck.

Shaping Your Story into a Defining Moment

The next step is to begin shaping your transcript into an essay. The Defining Moment story provides an accessible and straightforward skeleton for college application essays. All of the new Common Application prompts, as well as the other types of essays—influences, issues, community, why I want to go to this college or major in this program—can be answered using Defining Moment stories. Defining Moment stories can be used to shape many other types of application essays and cover letters as well. No matter what the essay question, you can almost always find a possible answer by asking yourself, "Where are the moments in my life that show the reader what I want them to know about me?"

Here are some tips for working with your Defining Moment stories and turning them into successful college application essays:

1. **Clarify which type of moment it is.** Is it an achievement, a dilemma, a risk, or some other type of significant experience?
2. **Achievements tend to make the least compelling essays for the reader.** And your achievements are probably included in other parts of your application. What else is important about this story, other than your working hard and achieving what you set out to achieve?
3. **Successful essays happen in the world, not in your thoughts.** If you are writing about your own change, what actions in the world can be used to show that change?
4. **Avoid putting a conclusion or moral at the end.** For instance, you do not need to say "That was how I knew I wanted to major in Applied Math." A successful Defining Moment story will show your learning, so you do not need to say it again.

In the next two exercises you will work with your Defining Moment story and develop specific elements of a successful essay.

Highlighting Strengths

You will need highlighters of four different colors for this exercise (yellow, green, orange, and blue). It really helps to print the essay out and do this exercise with a hard copy. Note that there may be places where colors overlap.

Read your essay out loud from the transcription and answer the following questions:

> **Where is the story strongest?** Highlight in green those places where the story is strongest. Where is the action? Where do other people enter the story? Highlight in yellow the scripts and generalizations, places where you feel the story could be stronger and want to bring out more details in your story.
> **Where is my voice strongest?** Highlight in blue the places that sound like your unique spoken voice. Highlight in orange the places where you feel your voice could be stronger and more unique.

If you are working on this exercise with a partner, give that person a hard copy of your essay and have that partner complete this exercise on your essay and also on his or her own. Either in discussion with your partner or on your own, write out answers to the following questions:

1. What are the qualities that make the strong parts of your essay stand out?

_____

_____

_____

_____

_____

2. Did you and your partner agree about the essay's strengths? If yes, what are they? If not, what did each of you see as strengths?

_____

_____

_____

_____

_____

3. Did you and your partner see the same areas that can be strengthened? If yes, what are they? If not, what did each of you see?

_____

_____

_____

_____

_____

In the next exercise you are going to extract the strongest parts of your transcribed story, leave the rest behind, and begin to expand the areas that are strongest by exploring them in greater depth. This may feel a bit scary at first (or it may feel fabulously exhilarating). You want to get comfortable with this gesture: take what is strongest and build on it, and let the rest go. In any case, you don't need to worry: you are doing the cutting in a separate file, so you can always go back to the old version if you want it for reference.

EXERCISE 3

Contract to Expand

This exercise has two steps: contract and expand. Take the file of your transcribed story and make an electronic copy.

1. Contract

First, you are going to delete any part of the essay not highlighted in one of the four colors.

2. Expand

Any place you have yellow (general scripts) or orange (bland voice) highlighting, imagine you are a stranger reading your story, and answer the following questions:

> Where is this part of the story going?
> What is missing?
> What would make this part of the story more my own?

And then, for each of the yellow and orange sections, write down at least three specific ideas about how to make that part of the story stronger and more specific. You can add comments either in the electronic copy or with sticky notes on the hard copy.

Making Revisions

Remember: you are not "editing" your essay; for right now you are exploring different ways to expand it and make it more specific. Your story will get longer, but don't worry about the length for now. It is always easier to prune your essay back to 650 words or 250 words—or even 1,000 characters—when you have a variety of details to choose from. In the next exercise, Revision Decisions, you will sift through these details and make a plan to shape the next draft of your essay.

EXERCISE 4

Revision Decisions

Looking back through the work you did in this chapter, and your discussions with other people who are going through this process, you are going to decide which are the strengths of the essay you want to build on, and which specific parts you want to develop further.

What are the strengths of your essay?

1. _____

2. _____

3. _____

What else do you want your reader to know about you from this essay?

1. _____

2. _____

3. _____

What is the most important thing you want to achieve in your revision of this essay?

_____

_____

_____

Remember you cannot do everything, and certainly not at once. So each time you revise an essay, it is much better to work with a sense of curiosity and building on what works best, rather than "fixing" what is wrong.

Thinking About Majors: High School vs. College Thinking

This has probably happened to you: you arrive at class, let's say it's science class, and you realize that you've grabbed the wrong notebook and you're stuck with your history notes. You tear out a clean sheet of paper, put your history notebook back into your bag, and look over a friend's shoulder. But what if your history notes could be relevant to your science class?

You may be thinking that's not really possible: there's a class for history and a class for science . . . and ne'er the twain shall meet. But when you get to college—especially in liberal arts colleges and cross-disciplinary programs across majors—you'll find that your courses relate to one another in surprising and meaningful ways. For example, did you learn about the DNA model in biology? Did you learn how that model came to be? Biophysicists Francis Crick, James D. Watson, and Rosalind Franklin discovered the double helix in 1953, but only Crick and Watson published the findings and received credit for the hypothesis. Franklin, however, contributed the data that Crick and Watson used to construct the double helix.[2] To understand what really went on, you need to know about how women were treated in the 1950s. How did World War II change things for women? How prevalent was sexism? What was a woman's role in society? You might need to dig up those history notes after all!

These connections will be the backbone of your college education. No matter which major you pick, you will encounter a variety of subjects on your academic journey. As you discover where your interests lie, you will learn to approach the questions that matter to you most from a variety of perspectives. When thinking about your major, remember that academic subjects are not self-contained systems. You'll figure out how history and science, or maybe science and literature, or even math and art, can work together to enrich your knowledge.

If you think about college as a journey, your major (which is college shorthand for your major field of study) will be one of your main pathways through college, with lots of smaller routes and surprising turns off the main road. More than 60 percent of students change their majors at least once after they arrive at college.[3] But it is still a tremendously useful exercise to "try on" different college majors during the college process and to think about what life would be like if each of them were your main course of study in college. Talk to students who have that major—about their courses, internships, and career ambitions. Read articles about the field, including articles written by the professors you might study with at each college. What are the important trends in that field? What is the school's focus within that field? What type of research might you be involved in if you worked with a professor as an undergraduate? Is this a field that requires graduate school or other training to advance professionally? The more you explore these questions in advance, the more likely you are to find majors—and colleges—that are a great fit for you, and to take advantage of all the different types of learning that college has for you to explore.

Sample Essay from a Defining Moment Transcript

You will do much better work if you focus on just one or two things for each round of revisions. Here is an example of how one student expanded his Defining Moment into a completed essay.

BEFORE

Is change really that difficult? I thought so! I never was the type to accept change, but instead I cursed it. Change always came when I had least expected it. When I got used to one thing, it changed to something completely different. Why adjust when eventually I will have to change again? I thought that change was useless. But then I saw first-hand how change could be positive. It was my older brother, Shane, who showed me.

Growing up in the Bronx is not easy. I am a witness to the life of someone who got caught up in the wrong crowd and ended up joining a gang due to peer pressure. I remember on one dark winter day, Shane had been attacked. We had gone on a retreat with our church for a weekend, and while on the beach, surrounding a campfire Shane felt a strong conviction that he needed to turn his life around. From that moment he decided that he had no true purpose in the gang life, and that lifestyle wasn't right for him anymore. Shane realized that this lifestyle was only surrounded by negativity, and he wanted to be a positive influence for his younger brothers. His life helped me to see just how much the positive outweighed the negative in my life. Through Shane's motivation to change his lifestyle, I have been influenced to be an inspiration to not only myself, but to the world around me.

I learned to speak up, go out, and be the change in my community, standing up for what I believe in. Whether it is spending time investing in the lives of others, or just feeding the hungry homeless man across the street, I know that I can make an impact. Also, having the opportunity to mentor children at a local after-school has made me proud because I have a chance to represent a positive figure in the lives of children who may have never seen positivity before. One child in particular said to me once, "the world just needs to be a better place Mr. Jay." I agreed and said that the world does need to be a better place, and the change begins with us. I have learned to guide others with the confidence that I had learned in my years watching Shane protecting me and my younger brother.

Being an agent of change in my community isn't just a commitment for me, it is a lifestyle. Right now, I live in a community where crime rates are consistently high. I live in a community where graduation rates are decreasing while incarceration rates are increasing. I live in a community where everyone settles with just the bare minimum. I wake up every morning with a clear vision of the future. In this vision, I see a community where service and involvement are major trends. I see a community where education and graduation are priorities instead of a privilege. I see a community where the bare minimum isn't the standard, but everyone goes far beyond it. This lifestyle I have learned to live will be carried with me wherever I go, and I will apply what I have learned to whatever I do. I have learned to view my community and my role in my community in a positive way instead of negative, and I owe this to the example set by my brother, Shane. Qualities that I now possess, such as learning to put the needs of others before my own, will help me as I continue on this journey toward success.

AFTER

I want to be a light in the darkness; someone who stands out against the "norm." I want to be the difference maker, who stands up for change. I understand that change takes one step at a time, but it's up to everyone to make a first step of his own. My older brother, Shane, did, which showed me that I could too.

I remember on one dark winter day, Shane had been attacked by a rival gang. A few weeks later, we went on a retreat with our church. While on this retreat, we visited the beach and started a bright campfire. As we gazed upon the fire all we heard was our youth pastor's voice saying, "Tonight's the night of change, tonight's the night to let burdens go." He told us to write our struggles down on a piece of paper, and when we felt ready we were to throw it into the fire. As tears rolled down Shane's face, he got up and threw his paper in the fire. I watched as the flames devoured his pledge to the gang, and that night Shane committed himself to living a new life.

That night I changed too. I realized that I could impact others. Each week after school, I volunteer at a local after-school program, where I help students with their homework. After they finish, I set up laptop computers and run my version of a "Computer 101" class. During this time, I have the opportunity to interact with the students, as well as a chance to learn from them. Malik, a 12-year-old student in the after-school program, once said to me, "The world just needs to be a better place, Mr. Jay." As I agreed, I replied, "The world does need to be a better place, and it's up to us to change it." My brother, Shane, didn't have a positive role model before joining a gang. As "Mr. Jay," I have the chance to be this role model for students like Malik, who may have never had a positive role model before.

Being an agent of change in my community isn't just a cliché for me, it's a necessary commitment. Right now, I live in a community where crime rates are consistently high, where graduation rates are decreasing while incarceration rates are increasing. I live in a community where everyone settles with just the bare minimum. In my vision of the future, I see a community where service and involvement are a regular part of everyone's schedule, and not just a pop-in activity around the holidays. I see a community where education and graduation are priorities instead of a privilege. I see a community where the bare minimum isn't the standard, but everyone goes far beyond it. All of this started with Shane changing his direction around a campfire, which helped me to see a world of possibilities. Now I am stepping out in faith in order to help others to see my vision with me.

—JOEL BURT-MILLER (Brandeis University '16)

At this point you have a rough draft and the materials you need to shape your Defining Moment story into the core of a successful college application essay:

> You have focused on the story's strengths.
> You have taken out the filler and anything else that does not move the story forward.
> You have explored ways to expand the story where it is still vague and general.
> You have chosen a goal to focus your revision.

In the next two chapters—Chapter 7: Focus Out and Chapter 8: Map It—you will complete a second draft of this Defining Moment essay by focusing first on the world in which the story occurs and then on the essay's structure. If you find yourself getting impatient and wanting to rush to the end, I urge you to let your pace stay slow for just a little longer. The next two chapters add specific skills from the world of fiction that you may not be accustomed to or even aware of. By learning these tools, and working through them as separate skills, you will be able to build on them—not only as the structural elements of confident college application essays, but also as key building blocks of successful interviews and public speaking.

Further Reading

Cron, Lisa. *Wired for Story.* Berkeley, CA: Ten Speed Press, 2012.

Guber, Peter. *Tell to Win: Connect, Persuade, and Triumph with the Hidden Power of Story.* New York: Crown Business, 2011.

CHAPTER 7

Focus Out

A mountain is composed of tiny grains of earth. The ocean is made up of tiny drops of water. . . . Life is but an endless series of details, actions, speeches, and thoughts. And the consequences whether good or bad of even the least of them are far-reaching.

—SIVANANDA[1]

One of the hardest parts of the Moments Method for many students is expressing their thoughts and feelings without saying, "I felt . . ." or "I was. . . ." In this chapter you will learn how to get your essays out of your mind and into the world of shared experience. Whenever you show other people your experience, you invite them to share your emotions and empathize with you. When you tell them what you felt, on the other hand, you lose the power to connect with them.

REFRESH

What Do Emotions Look Like?

What is an emotion you experience a lot? There's no right or wrong answer, and no one is watching, so pick the first or second idea that comes to mind. Write that emotion in the center of the page, just beneath these directions, and then write as many details as you can about experiencing that emotion. Be very specific. Where and how does the emotion start? What is the experience like to you? What do you do? What can others see? Do you recognize that emotion in others? Set a timer and free write for five minutes or more, keeping your pen moving or your fingers typing.

One Story Two Ways

Read the following two stories:

> My father died when I was a junior in high school. I never really thought about him dying, right up to the day he died, so it was a huge shock and loss to me. I had taken care of him the whole time he was sick, and my mother was working to keep the family together so she really wasn't home very much. My father really believed in me as a writer and told me that he wanted me to finish his book about cancer if he wasn't able to. My father is my inspiration as I apply to college.

> It was February 7, 1975, and I told my boyfriend Ed, "You can come over later." My father was sitting in the living room. His legs were yellow and swollen, his stomach bloated. When I went to kiss him his breath smelled like he hadn't brushed his teeth, and I turned my cheek away. "Can I get you anything, Daddy?" I asked.
>
> "No, I feel great now that you're home. But there's something important I have to tell you"
>
> "What's that?"
>
> "If I don't live to finish this book about beating cancer, I want you to finish it for me."

Describe the way each of the stories affects you. Where and how do you experience the two stories? What do you remember from your own experience reading each of them? Which one are you more likely to remember a few hours or a few days later? What will you remember?

_____

_____

_____

_____

_____

_____

_____

When you are shaping your stories into essays, whenever you find yourself straying into scripts and generalizations—phrases like "That was the day I realized that all people are equal"—stop right there! Before you go any further, ask yourself, "How can I open up the story so others can experience what happened from my point of view?" What did you do that day, or the next day, to act on your realization about equality? What did you say when your newfound conviction was challenged by someone with more hierarchical thinking? What difference did your insight make when you encountered inequality in your everyday world? How would someone else know that you had this change in worldview? If you took action, that is a story. If you wrote a blog about it, that is a story—a published story, even better! If you spoke with someone, that is a story. But things that happen in your mind—"I realized," "I figured out," or "I felt"—those are all opportunities to draw your reader closer by getting outside of your thoughts and focusing on the world of shared experience.

This pause to take something that happens in your own mind and shape it into something other people can experience and share will make all of your communications richer and more powerful—for you and everyone you converse with, in speech and in writing. Imagine a world where everyone spoke specifically about what they experienced, rather than, "Well it was, you know, kind of, sort of really awesome, and I learned so much."

The Three *D*'s: Details, Dialogue, and Description

To get out of your own thoughts and into the world of shared experience, in this chapter you will use details, dialogue, and description to draw your reader into your experience and leave him or her wanting to know more about you. Details, dialogue, and description make your writing vivid and memorable. The three *D*'s add unique character to your writing, just as surely as different vegetables and spices make one soup a minestrone and another one pasta e fagioli. Here's how to do it:

> **Details:** Draw the reader into the moment with vivid sensory details: What colors were the leaves? What sounds came with the pounding rain? Which vegetables could you taste in your grandmother's soup? What perfume was she wearing? Those scratchy trousers you wore to your first interview—were they polyester or wool? Some people remember all sorts of details; other people's memories are a bit fuzzy and vague. If you find it hard to remember details, focus on the present. Take even one hour a day to tune into the world around you, and you will start to notice more details. Writing the details down will reinforce and speed up your learning.

> **Dialogue:** Re-creating the exact words of a conversation is extremely powerful. Which of these two examples draws you in and makes you want to read more?

We talked about Manhattanhenge.

or

"That is the biggest sun I have ever seen," Charles said, pointing west across 53rd Street.

As humans we love to hear the actual words people say. Your essay instantly becomes more intimate when you include dialogue; it is almost as if we are eavesdropping on two people's private conversation when you quote their exact words in your essay. So learn to note the exact words people say and write down how different people talk—including their accents, their uncanny choice of words, and the things they say in other languages. Write it down exactly as you hear it, just as you did with your own story.

> **Description:** Use the journalist's questions: *who, what, when, where*, with the occasional *why* woven in. What year was it? What season? What was going on historically? Who else was there? Set the scene for your reader, so he or she is ready when you appear and take action. The more precise you can be, the more powerfully you will connect with your reader, drawing that person into the action at a very visceral and personal level.

Working with Quotations

Dialogue is a great way to show the reader what is happening without summarizing and interpreting the action of the story. Dialogue can also be used to expand the action, using your own words and the words of others.

HELPFUL QUESTIONS TO CAPTURE DIALOGUE
What do you want to convey through dialogue?
What do other characters in the story reveal through their words?
What were the exact words, expressions, and even languages used by different people in the story?

TYPES OF DIALOGUE
1. Conversation
   I asked, "How was your day, Dad?" And my father replied, "Son, we got some really bad news."
2. Description
   I told Sally, "The moon looks like a big, old peach tonight," and she smiled.
3. Interjection
   "Don't take my iPod away! I promise to do my homework right after school next time," John pleaded. When John broke his promise the next day, I said, "I know Dad's not here now, but you need to follow his rules."
4. Comment
   Coach said, "There's not much we can do to win now." I pleaded with him, "What about that end around play we practiced last week? Let's give that a try."

HOW TO FORMAT DIALOGUE IN YOUR ESSAY

1. What the person said—exactly—goes inside quotation marks.
   Carol said, "You must include the exact words the person says."
   a. Introduce the quotation with a comma (,) or colon (:).
   b. In American English, punctuation goes inside quotation marks.
2. If you have a quotation inside a quotation, here's how the punctuation works:
   Carol urged us on with these words: "My father always said, 'Everyone makes mistakes; smart people learn from their mistakes.'"

GRAMMAR RULES FOR DIALOGUE

> The exact words of a speaker are put in quotation marks.
> Quotation marks always come in pairs. If there are opening quotation marks, there must be closing quotation marks as well.
> The first letter of a direct quote is always capitalized, when the quoted material is a complete sentence.
> If a direct quotation is interrupted mid-sentence, the second part of the quotation should not be capitalized unless it is a proper noun: *"I found out," explained Jim, "that I am not an only child."*
> Use quotation marks only at the beginning and end of quoted material, not at the beginning or end of each sentence.
> Separate quoted material from the speaker with commas: *She said, "Don't bother me, Peter.";* *"We sat around," said the boys, "and read books all day."*
> If you are introducing a new speaker to the dialogue, begin with identifying the speaker: *Andrea spoke quietly, "I'm here."*
> Every time there is a new speaker, start a new paragraph, even if the speaker only says one word.

EXERCISE 2

The Three *D*'s in Everyday Life

Before you begin adding details, dialogue, and description to your Defining Moment story, take a day to explore the details you find in everyday life:

What do you see, hear, smell, taste and touch at three different places? You can include home, school, your transportation to school, a friend's house, basketball practice, or play rehearsal. Anything is fine. Just pick three places and include at least 10 sensory details for each place.

Place 1: _____

1. _____
2. _____
3. _____
4. _____
5. _____
6. _____
7. _____
8. _____
9. _____
10. _____

_____

_____

Place 2: _____

1. _____
2. _____
3. _____
4. _____
5. _____
6. _____
7. _____
8. _____
9. _____
10. _____

_____

_____

Place 3: _____

1. _____
2. _____
3. _____
4. _____
5. _____
6. _____
7. _____
8. _____
9. _____
10. _____

_____
_____

Observe one conversation between two or more people (not yourself). Note any particular words or phrases that each of the people uses. Watch their facial expressions. Can you figure out what they are feeling from their words and facial expressions? Do you observe that there are things they do not say? How else do they communicate?

_____
_____
_____
_____
_____

Finally, pick a part of the day that you usually ignore, something you go through almost on autopilot (perhaps your bus ride to school or your family dinner), and write down at least 10 things you notice about the scene. This can be as simple as what people are wearing or eating, but look closely. Are their shoes muddy or worn? Is the table set the usual way or is something different today? Just observe, and when you have a chance write your list down here.

1. _____
2. _____
3. _____

4. _____

5. _____

6. _____

7. _____

8. _____

9. _____

10. _____

_____

_____

Expanding Your Story with the Three *D*'s

Now take another look at your Defining Moment essay draft from Chapter 6: Write It Out, and ask yourself:

> What are the story's three to five most memorable details?

_____

_____

_____

_____

_____

> How does the writer change or grow?

_____

_____

_____

_____

> What else can you do to help the reader experience the writer's growth or change?

_____

_____

_____

_____

Slowing the Action Down

Next divide your Defining Moment essay into a series of five to eight discrete actions, almost like a recipe or a task list. First put each of the story's actions on a separate line in the first box. Then, you will unpack the specific moments of your Defining Moment essay by exploring sensory details, dialogue, and physical description for each one in the following boxes.

Moment by Moment

MOMENTS

List the key moments of your story.

EXAMPLE: _I walked into my new high school._

1. _____

2. _____

3. _____

4. _____

5. _____

6. _____

7. _____

8. _____

SENSORY DETAILS

What did you see, hear, smell, taste, and touch?

EXAMPLE: *I put pennies in my new loafers and wore them without socks.*

1. _____

2. _____

3. _____

4. _____

5. _____

6. _____

7. _____

8. _____

DIALOGUE

What did people say?

EXAMPLE: *"You are going to get in trouble," Sue whispered. "Socks are part of the dress code."*

1. _____

2. _____

3. _____

4. _____

5. _____

6. _____

7. _____

8. _____

Who else was there? Where are you? What marks the time and place?

EXAMPLE: *In Mississippi school starts in August. It was over 100 degrees outside, and my school had no air conditioning.*

1. _____

2. _____

3. _____

4. _____

5. _____

6. _____

7. _____

8. _____

The Community Essay

To practice focusing out you are going to shape another one of your stories to answer a question that you will almost certainly need in your supplement essays and interviews—the Community Essay. This essay will also help you describe the communities that have shaped your way of being in the world and how those communities have shaped you and what you uniquely bring to your college community.

How do you show the community you come from? How do you convey that you see yourself as part of that community but also different in some ways? How do you talk about your past communities in a way that also conveys your aspirations about the future? Here's one student's story about his best friend:

> It was late at night, and I was finishing my English paper. I looked down and there was a Facebook message from my friend Amar, who dropped out of school when his girlfriend got pregnant. "Jakob," it said, "we just had our baby girl. What do you think we should name her?"
>
> "Give me a few minutes. I'll find you some names." I wanted her to have a name that was powerful and proud. I started searching on the Internet. I'm not even sure how long it was; I got lost in sites about Greek mythology and Hindu mysticism.

At least once my mother walked by and said, "Jakob, are you working on your paper or are you playing video games?"

"I'm working, Mom."

After a while I wrote back, "Amar, I found you two names: Serena or Jade. They are both green names, green like my favorite color."

"Those are great names. Where did you find them, man?"

"I love research like you love your daughter. Gotta go. I'll stop by tomorrow."

That short story (less than 200 words) tells you a lot about the community Jakob comes from, and what makes him different from his friend. His guidance counselor told him not to write about Facebook and his late night excursions through the bowels of the Internet. She said, "Definitely do not write about your friend getting his girlfriend pregnant. That will not make you look good." But this is Jakob's world; this story reveals who he is. When you read this essay you experience how he is both connected to that world and yearning, searching for something else. Now you are going to try it.

EXERCISE 5

Community Essay Brainstorming

In their supplements colleges often ask students some version of the following: A range of academic interests, personal perspectives, and life experiences adds much to the educational mix. Given your personal background, describe an experience that illustrates what you would bring to the diversity in a college community or an encounter that demonstrates the importance of diversity to you. What are the first things you think of?

What You Bring to Your Local Community

_____

_____

_____

_____

_____

What You Bring to a College Community

_____

_____

_____

_____

_____

What You Bring to a Global Community

_____

_____

_____

_____

_____

The Community Essay: Tips and Tools

The Community Essay is an opportunity to show people what community means to you, how you make a difference in your community today, and how you plan to make a difference in your college community. Here are some tips and tools to expand your thinking about community:

1. **What does community mean to you?** Is there a story or moment that conveys your ideal of community?
2. **Consider what you bring to different types of community**—your local community, your college community, and the global community.
3. *Diversity* **is a word that is used a lot and means different things to different people.** What is your personal definition of *diversity*—in 10 words or less? Which moments from your own experience show this definition and bring it to life for other people?
4. **What have your family and community taught you about diversity?** Get past the obvious here, and explore things that you usually take for granted. For instance, perhaps your family has adopted a child from Ethiopia. Maybe you attend a school that has students from many different neighborhoods, or your parents were born in two different parts of the world.
5. **Avoid political labels and grandstanding.** You should not use an essay about community (or diversity) as an opportunity to take political positions or expound on your religious beliefs. Instead, choose a moment that shows some aspect of your place and

purpose in the community. It's fine to show yourself in action in a political or religious part of your life; just don't tell people what you think (that would be a script). Perhaps you have been a political organizer in your community. If so, you can take us to the heart of that work and show us what you did and whose lives were affected. But no distant proclamations or ideals that come from outside your own experience.

6. **There are words and phrases to avoid.** *I'm very open. I am colorblind. Diverse. Different. I am the only. . . . I have always. . . .*

The Community Question

Among many other roles, colleges are communities. Many colleges ask questions about community to get a sense of the communities that shaped you, and what you see as your role in the community. There are many different versions of the community question, and they often ask you to talk about yourself in relation to the community, or to describe what you bring to the campus community.

Here are some examples of the community question you might find on the supplements for different colleges:

> Community—educational, geographic, religious, political, ethnic, or other—can define an individual's experience and influence THEIR journey. How has your community, as you identify it, shaped your perspective? (Barnard College)

> Write about an experience in which you encountered a tension between personal freedom and community standards. Discuss the experience and the underlying issues, how you dealt with the tension, and whether or not there was a satisfactory resolution. (Haverford College)

> If you had the complete attention of your community for five minutes, what would you say, and what would you hope to accomplish? (Pomona College)

> Everyone belongs to many different communities and/or groups defined by (among other things) shared geography, religion, ethnicity, income, cuisine, interest, race, ideology, or intellectual heritage. Choose one of the communities to which you belong, and describe that community and your place within it. (University of Michigan)

> The quality of Rice's academic life and the Residential College System are heavily influenced by the unique life experiences and cultural traditions each student brings. What perspective do you feel that you will contribute to life at Rice? (Rice University)

> One of the fascinating qualities of Grinnell College is the diversity of its student body. Grinnell students come from around the world and from innumerable socio-economic, religious, and cultural backgrounds. What place, people, or culture would you like to get to know better and why? (Grinnell College)

Whether or not you answer the community question, it is helpful to ask yourself about different colleges, "What would it be like to be a member of this community?"

Community Moments

Step 1

From Exercise 5: Community Essay Brainstorming choose three ways you contribute to your community and list them here.

Contribution 1 _____

Contribution 2 _____

Contribution 3 _____

Step 2

Describe moments that show the ways you contribute to your community.

Contribution 1 Moments

1. _____

2. _____

3. _____

Contribution 2 Moments

1. _____

2. _____

3. _____

Contribution 3 Moments

1. _____

2. _____

3. _____

Step 3

Choose a moment from Step 2, tell the story out loud (three minutes), and transcribe it.

When you are completing this essay for different college applications, research what diversity means to each of them. Do you feel like you would fit in with each community? Do they have clubs or other activities that foster the type of community you believe in? What do current students say? This is very important for your happiness in college. Take the time to ask this question about every college you are considering.

Three Things to Look For

There are three types of programs that are increasingly important to learn the skills you will need to succeed in a global workforce. These programs distinguish universities from one another, and are worth considering closely.

Study Abroad

Many students take a semester or year abroad during their sophomore or junior year of college. If studying abroad is part of your college vision, you should start planning well in advance. Following are some questions to explore:

> What is your college major/minor going to be?
> Which country/program will best fit into your academic plan?
> Which languages are you studying?
> Do you want language immersion? Community service abroad?

At the beginning of sophomore year—or sooner—make an appointment with your college's study abroad office. Ask if your college sponsors any programs abroad. When applying to study abroad programs, you generally have two choices:

1. You can go on a program that's run by a university or outside organization like IES Abroad (www.iesabroad.org).

   OR

2. You can apply directly to a university as a visiting student.

Talk to your study abroad advisor and to your professors and academic advisors about which program will best fit with your educational and professional goals.

If you receive financial aid, your school is obligated to transfer at least 75 percent of your financial aid package to your tuition abroad. But you may be required to pay the rest. Be sure to file a FAFSA and take care of any paperwork your school requires.

Resources

If you are thinking about studying abroad, check out these resources:

> Touch base with the US State Department for all of your travel needs:
>   http://travel.state.gov/. (They also have a free iPhone/Android app!)
> Read reviews of study abroad programs and check out scholarships:
>   www.studyabroad101.com/ and www.goabroad.com/.
> The *Lonely Planet* guides are aimed at students and are really comprehensive.
>   They probably have a guide for your destination: www.lonelyplanet.com/.
> Here are some recommended iPhone and Android apps for your travel:
>   http://mashable.com/2013/01/16/apps-for-studying-abroad/.

Internships

Internships, in the summer or during the academic year, are crucial for college students. Many students' internships turn into real jobs down the road. You will want to take advantage of the resources your college provides, especially if there is a career office or an alumni network you can tap into for advice. You can send out one résumé to a variety of different internships but don't forget to customize your cover letter for each position you are applying to. Follow all application directions! Before an interview, ask a parent, professor, or counselor to work with you on a mock interview, and write down answers to questions you are anticipating. Don't be afraid to cold contact a company that interests you!

Resources

> Résumé and Cover Letter: Harvard has great resources:
>   www.ocs.fas.harvard.edu/students/jobs_resume.htm.
> Two *Forbes* articles about networking and interviewing:
>   www.forbes.com/sites/francesbridges/2012/05/31/how-to-get-an-awesome
>   -internship/ and www.forbes.com/sites/francesbridges/2012/05/31/how-to
>   -get-an-awesome-internship/2.
> Idealist is a great place to look for nonprofit internship listings: www.idealist.org.

Work Study

Work study may be a part of your financial aid package; 3,400 schools participate in the program. When you fill out your Free Application for Federal Student Aid (FAFSA), indicate your interest in the work study program. Also make sure you apply to your college's work study program as soon as the application becomes available. Since the program is part of government aid, you have to receive more than federal minimum wage, but you can only work a certain number of hours per week. Your employer may be your school, or it may be a private nonprofit organization in the neighborhood (7 percent of work study positions must help the community in some way). The program tries to match students with jobs that match their academic interests.

Further Reading

Clark, Tim, Osterwalder, Alexander, and Yves Pigneur. *Business Model You*. Hoboken, NJ: John Wiley and Sons, 2012.

Gardner, Howard. *Five Minds for the Future*. Cambridge, Mass.: Harvard Business School Press, 2006.

Savitz-Romer, Mandy, and Suzanne M. Bouffard. *Ready, Willing, and Able: A Developmental Approach to College Access and Success*. Cambridge, Mass.: Harvard Education Press, 2012.

CHAPTER 8

Map It

*A map does not just chart, it unlocks and formulates meaning;
it forms bridges between here and there, between disparate
ideas that we did not know were previously connected.*

—REIF LARSEN, THE SELECTED WORKS OF T. S. SPIVET[1]

The final step of shaping a spoken story into a written essay is to map it. Remember when we talked about the difference between a critical essay, with its introduction-examples-conclusion structure, and a personal essay, which is structured as a story? (See the Critical Essays vs. Personal Essays sidebar in Chapter 3.) In this chapter you will learn the elements of personal story structure. In later chapters you will work with some additional maps that can be used, specifically, to shape essays about influences (Chapter 10: Explore Perspectives) and issues (Chapter 11: Raise the Stakes). But the map you learn in this chapter always works. You can come back to this structure again and again, every time that you need to take the ebb and flow of actual experience and shape it into a story that shows who you are and what you can be counted on to do in college, work, or relationships.

Drawing Your Map

A map tells us where we are going. It is a visual representation of a journey from one place to another. Even if there's a subway that's closed or a road that has traffic, the map reminds us of where we're going—where the story begins, where it twists and turns, and where it ends. In this chapter you will learn how to build an essay with a clear sense of purpose. The action of the story—the story's structure, or map—will reveal the purpose, so you do not have to tell the reader why this experience has been important to you. Your story will remain in the action and in the moment, start to finish, and your reader will experience

REFRESH

Lost and Found

For at least five minutes, keeping your pen moving or your fingers typing, free write about a time you got lost.

your Defining Moment side by side with you. Recall the three-sentence story from Chapter 3: Transform Scripts to Stories. In the next series of exercises you are going to use the three-sentence story in a variety of new ways to complete the process of shaping your spoken story into a written essay.

Think of your story as having three beats—the beginning, the middle, and the end. You can count them: one, two, three. We call the beginning the *Magnet* because it draws the reader into your story. We call the middle the *Pivot* because something changes. And we call the end the *Glow* because it leaves the reader with a memory of you. In Chapter 9 you will work specifically on the Magnet and Glow; here you will learn how to build tight and emotionally resonant stories based on variations of this three-beat story structure. It's like the steady beat of your favorite song. It is there in the background, and everything else builds and grows around it.

EXERCISE 1

Story Order

Choose a new story from your Story Portfolio (see Chapter 3). And list everything that happens in the story, in the order that it happens.

_____

_____

_____

_____

_____

_____

_____

_____

_____

_____

_____

_____

_____

The next step is to choose—from all the different moments of the story, from everything that happens—the beginning, middle, and end of your story.

Choosing Order

First, go back to Exercise 1: Story Order, and circle the three moments that for you are the beginning, middle, and end, and then write them below.

Beginning: _____

Why is this the beginning? _____

_____

_____

Middle: _____

Why is this the middle? _____

_____

_____

End: _____

Why is this the end? _____

_____

_____

Are there any other moments that were important, but you are not sure if they are the beginning, middle, or end? Write those down here.

_____

_____

_____

_____

Defining Moment Map

Now copy your beginning, middle, and end from Exercise 2: Choosing Order onto the following Defining Moment Map as your Magnet, Pivot, and Glow.

MAGNET

↓

PIVOT

↓

GLOW

THEMES/IDEAS TO EXPLORE FURTHER

Magnet, Pivot, and Glow

Next we are going to take some time to explore each of the three sections of your Defining Moment Map, starting at the end and working back to the beginning.

> Start with the Glow, the end of the story. What is the very last action of the story? Write that down in the box labeled "Glow" in Exercise 3: Defining Moment Map.
> What Pivot, or change of action, in the middle of the story drives the story to that ending? Write that moment of change in the middle box labeled "Pivot."
> Finally where does the story of that change leading to that ending begin? Write the beginning down in the box labeled "Magnet."
> This mapping exercise often generates a lot of ideas and creative thinking! The box at the bottom labeled "Themes/Ideas to Explore Further" is a place to jot down anything that comes up while you are mapping: ideas about the story's importance or theme, parts of the told story that you decide not to use here but may work somewhere else, or any other ideas that you discover while mapping.

These three moments—Magnet, Pivot, and Glow—may be close together or they may be spread out over time. You are shaping a Defining Moment story, and in order to show your reader that you have changed—or learned or discovered or made a difference—you need to show the reader moments before and after the change.

Finally, go back and explore each of the three moments with the tools you learned in Chapter 7: Focus Out. Focusing on the three sections of your story in Exercise 3: Defining Moment Map, add as many details and as much dialogue and description as you can, almost as if each of those sections was its own story. Be very specific. Go back into each of those three moments of your story, explore what you find there, and write down as much as you can remember. What were people wearing? What did they say? What was usual about the moment, and what was unusual?

Congratulations, you have shaped another story! More than that, because you can use the Defining Moment Map to shape any story into a Defining Moment essay, you have learned a structure you can use to take the ebb and flow of any experience and shape it into an emotionally and intellectually successful essay to answer any question that college application essays or interviews throw your way.

Next we will explore some other ways you can use this sturdy, reliable three-beat structure to organize your essays. But first let's talk a bit more about order, and how different types of order work against one another in great writing. First, there is the order that the events happened in the world. We call that *story order*. Then there is the order in which the events happen on paper—the order that you read the events, the order they are revealed to you. We call that *reader's experience*. You can always tell the story in the same order that the events happened, but there are some curious things you can do to play story order off the reader's experience. Often, you can heighten the reader's experience by breaking down the story order and rearranging the story elements.

Here's an example. Every story has three beats, which we will number 1-2-3.

1. I went to the store.
2. I bought a dozen eggs.
3. I dropped them on the way home.

If you rearrange the elements, you have five more potential stories (1-3-2, 2-1-3, 2-3-1, 3-2-1, and 3-1-2). Now you are going to try this.

Scrambled Stories

Take another story from your Story Portfolio (see Chapter 3). Map out the story order using the Defining Moment Map.

```
┌─────────────────────────────────────────┐
│               MAGNET                      │
│                                           │
│                                           │
└─────────────────────────────────────────┘
                    ⬇
┌─────────────────────────────────────────┐
│               PIVOT                       │
│                                           │
│                                           │
└─────────────────────────────────────────┘
                    ⬇
┌─────────────────────────────────────────┐
│               GLOW                        │
│                                           │
│                                           │
└─────────────────────────────────────────┘
```

And now rearrange the story elements using the five other possible maps:

1 _____

3 _____

2 _____

2 _____

1 _____

3 _____

2 _____

3 _____

1 _____

3 _____

2 _____

1 _____

3 _____

1 _____

2 _____

What was revealed when you rearranged the story elements? Which order created the most suspense for the reader? Which order was the most powerful emotionally? Which characters and which actions seemed the most important in different versions of the story?

Students often say that the biggest challenge in completing a personal essay is getting everything you want to say into 650 words—or into 250 words or 150 words in shorter supplement essays. The fact is you never need to include everything. The last exercises have shown you how much you can do in three sentences—you can tell almost any experience in three compact sentences and make a lasting impression on your reader. So in every instance, when you feel you have too much information for one essay, at whatever length, focus on the three story elements, like three beats—Magnet, Pivot, Glow—and then focus on those three specific parts of the story. Next we are going to explore two very powerful ways to rearrange the story order to heighten the experience for the reader.

Combining Stories

In this exercise you will be combining two different moments to create one story with a Defining Moment structure.

1. First, pick two stories from your Story Portfolio (see Chapter 3) that you have not worked with before. Write the names of those two stories here.

   _____

   _____

2. Then map out the Magnet, Pivot, and Glow for each of the two stories.

   ### Story 1

   Magnet: _____

   Pivot: _____

   Glow: _____

   ### Story 2

   Magnet: _____

   Pivot: _____

   Glow: _____

3. Finally, taking two elements from one of the stories and one from the other story, create a Defining Moment Map that combines elements from the two stories into one. Pick the Glow first: where do you want your combined story to end? Then select the Pivot: where is the moment of change that moves toward that particular ending? And, finally, choose the Magnet: what is the best moment to draw the reader into your combined story? You won't be able to include all the details, but don't worry. Because the combined story has one three-beat structure, which the reader understands intuitively, your reader will follow you when you leap from one story to the next.[2]

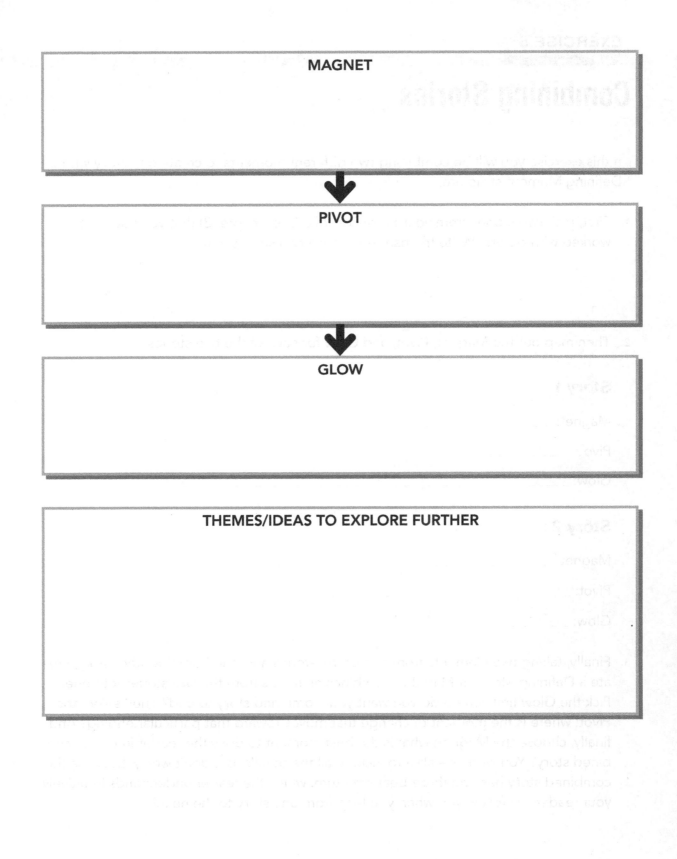

MAGNET

PIVOT

GLOW

THEMES/IDEAS TO EXPLORE FURTHER

4. Go ahead and flesh out the details of this new combined story on the Defining Moment Map, and then tell the story out loud, or write it or type it out.

_____

_____

_____

_____

_____

_____

_____

5. What were the strengths of the combined story? What were you able to do in this format that you could not have done with just one story or the other?

_____

_____

_____

_____

Inserting Another Story

From your Story Portfolio (see Chapter 3) pick two more stories:

_____

_____

Working backward from the end of each story, map out the Magnet, Pivot, and Glow for each of the individual stories.

Story 1

Magnet: _____

Pivot: _____

Glow: _____

Story 2

Magnet: _____

Pivot: _____

Glow: _____

Then, in the following Defining Moment Map, take the Pivot from one story and insert it into the middle of the other story. Focus out to explore details for each of the combined moments. Then tell your story out loud or write it down.

```
┌─────────────────────────────────────────┐
│                  MAGNET                  │
│                                          │
│                                          │
│                                          │
└─────────────────────────────────────────┘
                     ↓
┌─────────────────────────────────────────┐
│                  PIVOT                   │
│                                          │
│                                          │
└─────────────────────────────────────────┘
                     ↓
┌─────────────────────────────────────────┐
│                  GLOW                    │
│                                          │
│                                          │
└─────────────────────────────────────────┘
```

Here is a college essay one student wrote combining two simple stories—a summer with her grandparents in Italy and making Italian dinner for her friends in New York—into one combined story.

New York City, 9 P.M. Friends are laughing in the next room squeezed around the dinner table, as I try to whip something up. I put the water to boil, adding salt. As I wait, the steam begins to twist, to twirl, filling up the kitchen. I pause to wipe the sweat from my brow.

At eight o'clock in the morning my shirt is already moist. Sweat rolls down my face, every inch of my body. A typical morning in Perugia.

Sauté the garlic in olive oil on medium heat.

The gravel in the driveway crunches and crackles, "E' arrivato zio Mario!" I run barefoot, almost tripping down the stairs, all the way to his car, arms outstretched. His hair, grayer this year, falls over his tanned face. His hands rest on his belt, one finger cut off above the joint. I pull on my boots and he climbs onto the tractor. He hauls me onto his lap holding me tightly. The tractor roars, an olive branch lightly grazes my face, the grasshoppers go silent. At the back of the field, Mario climbs up a ladder and starts trimming the tips of the branches, the polloni. I take them and pile them in heaps. The trees are brimming with olives this year.

Chop the tomatoes, put them to simmer with the garlic, add salt and pepper.

At noon, I walk back toward the house to find my nonna in the garden, wearing a flowered apron. She tells me puoi portarmi il cestino un po' più vicino? ("Bring that bucket a little closer, would you?") She fills it up with plump, juicy, purplish-red tomatoes, a meal in themselves.

Pour in the linguini, stir fresh basil into the tomatoes.

We break off stems of basil. Nonna says, vedi si devono prendere quelli pieni di fiori, così la pianta può crescere. ("See we have to take the ones with the most flowers on them, so the plant grows.") We climb the small hill with a full bucket of pomodori. It's hot.

Dice the mozzarella, strain the linguini, pour the sauce over them, and add the mozzarella.

I follow Nonna into the kitchen trying to avoid the gang of mothers, uncles, and aunts. I reach for the mozzarella and it melts in my mouth; creamy, smooth, dripping, flavor that overloads my senses. I thought I was so clever, but as I turn around, "Sarah can you set the table? And stop eating all the mozzarella!" They caught me. I take the tablemats and retreat to the step outside. The neighbor's cat rubs against my legs. I tear off a small piece of cheese and feed it to her.

Serve right out of the pot.

"Hey guys," I call over their laughter, "help me set the table, dinner is ready!"

—**SARAH SUTTO PLUNZ (Smith College '17)**

Story Order

Here are two specific types of story order you can explore as ways to heighten the relationship between action and emotion in your essays:

> **Begin in the middle.** Here the structure of your story is 2-1-3 (Pivot, Magnet, Glow) or 2-3-1 (Pivot, Glow, Magnet). The great thing about starting in the middle is you take your reader right into the action. Perhaps the Pivot is so powerful that you need to begin there to convey the story's importance. Then you can swing back to the beginning and end where the story actually ends, or finish the story and then end where the story actually began.

> **Begin at the end.** This story has a 3-2-1 (Glow, Pivot, Magnet) or 3-1-2 (Glow, Magnet, Pivot) structure. Perhaps the reader needs information from the end of the story to make sense of the beginning. Or perhaps the beginning is the most powerful element of the story, and you want to end with the beginning so that is the moment left in your reader's mind after reading your essay. Try starting your story at the end and working backward to the beginning, or start with the end and then jump back to the beginning and end with the moment of change.

Feel free to explore a variety of different ways to map your stories into essays. Perhaps you use different orders for different audiences, or to emphasize different elements of the same story to answer different types of questions.

Essay Topics That Work and Ones That Don't

Remember the three most important things college admissions officers look for in your essay are strong writing, a unique perspective, and an authentic voice:

> **Strong writing:** You want your writing to have a strong narrative thrust and to be written well. You should proofread your writing carefully for spelling and grammar, and only send essays that are examples of your best work.
> **Unique point of view:** Your essays should reveal your character, and what the world looks like from your perspective.
> **Authentic voice:** Sometimes students overedit their admissions essays until they sound very generic and bland. Stick to the qualities of your spoken voice, so it feels like you are in the room when someone reads your essay.

Some of the best essays come from everyday experiences that everyone can relate to: a family ritual, cooking, or a walk with a friend that has a surprising twist. If you have worked through the exercises in *Write Out Loud*, you have a wide variety of stories you can use to answer whatever questions get thrown at you in college admissions essays and interviews. But I often get asked, "Are there topics that are just off-limits?" Most topics from your own experience can be shaped into successful essays, but here are a few that tend to be big turnoffs and are bad choices for application essays:

First World problems: "Problems from living in a wealthy, industrialized nation that Third Worlders would probably roll their eyes at." (UrbanDictionary.com)

Flowery, self-consciously "artistic" writing: So throw away your thesaurus, and put your creative writing in your Arts Supplement.

Life as a spectator: Anything where you are watching others, rather than taking action yourself, is likely to fall flat.

TMI: Too much unfiltered emotion is usually, well, too much.

You have done a lot of work, and you have real tangible products to show for it:

> Life story (for EOP, HEOP, or QuestBridge)
> Story Portfolio
> Five or more essay drafts (three Defining Moments, Activity, Why College X, Community)
> Résumé
> Exploration of colleges and courses

You will use all of these elements to complete your college application essays. You are ready to start finishing your personal essay as well as your supplements to specific colleges. There is detailed information about how to complete all the nonessay sections of the Common Application in our *A Guide to the New 2013–2014 Common Application (CA4)*, which you will find at the end of this book and you can also access at www.storytocollege .com/writeoutloud.

The final exercise of this chapter brings together all the work you have done, so you have all of your stories—the heart and soul of your essays—on one chart you can access any time.

EXERCISE 7

Essay Options

From your Life in Moments, your Story Portfolio, and the work you have done so far in this book, use the following chart to pull together all of the stories you can use to complete different types of essays on college applications.

Types of Essays

What are my strongest essays? What are my next steps with each essay? First list all the possible stories you have to tell in each category.

_____

_____

_____

_____

_____

_____

_____

_____

Then pick three to five Defining Moments and one or two Issues, Influences, and Community stories that reveal key aspects of your character.

DEFINING MOMENTS

_____

_____

_____

_____

ISSUES

_____

_____

INFLUENCES

_____

_____

Then circle the stories you want to complete in Part 3: Perform to reveal key aspects of your character.

In the final section of *Write Out Loud*, Part 3: Perform, you will learn how to strengthen the beginning and end of each of your essays (Chapter 9: Magnet and Glow), how to write two more types of essays—the Influence Essay (Chapter 10: Explore Perspectives) and the Issues Essay (Chapter 11: Raise the Stakes), and how to maintain the power of your spoken voice in all of your writing (Chapter 12: Write Out Loud). You will also find grammar tips and interview tips in the final chapters.

Further Reading

Denning, Stephen. *The Springboard: How Storytelling Ignites Action in Knowledge-Era Organizations*. London and New York: Routledge, 2011.

Hart, Jack. *Storycraft: The Complete Guide to Writing Narrative Nonfiction*. Chicago: University of Chicago Press, 2011.

McKee, Robert. *Story: Substance, Structure, Style and the Principles of Screenwriting*. New York: ReganBooks, 1997.

PART 3

PERFORM

CHAPTER 9

Magnet and Glow

The beginnings and endings of all human undertakings are untidy.

—JOHN GALSWORTHY[1]

The final phase of the Moments Method is called Perform. You will learn how to complete successful application essays—for college or any other situation—by maintaining your spoken voice in your writing. I coined the phrase "performative writing" to describe this way of completing essays because it draws on tools from theater and improvisation to keep your writing alive and performing in the present with your audience.

The Successful Essay

Successful college application essays engage their readers right from the first sentence and leave them wanting to know more in the end. In this chapter you will learn how to strengthen the beginning (Magnet) and ending (Glow) of every essay you write, using the tools of personal storytelling and performance. In Chapter 5: Tell It Out Loud, you explored your college application essays as conversations with college admissions officers. We are going to push this framework further in the next chapters, showing you how to complete each essay as a specific performance for a specific audience.

Over the course of *Write Out Loud,* you have built a portfolio of stories that reveal crucial aspects of your character, moments when you changed or grew or made a difference. You may tell some of these same stories for other purposes—for a job interview, on a date, or just getting to know someone. A story always has an audience, and the audience shapes the performance. At the same time, your story changes that audience permanently. Whether or not you are admitted to that admissions officer's college, your life story becomes part

Last Summer

Many colleges ask, either in an essay or interview, "What did you do last summer?" Take 10 minutes and write down everything you did last summer. If you just hung out with your friends, write down their names, what they look like, and what counts as "hanging out." You get the idea. Just keep your pen moving or your fingers typing for 10 minutes.

of that person's experience. And each time someone reads your essay, it becomes part of that reader's experience. So when you are completing your essays, think of that process as performing your stories out loud to a live audience. Each finished essay is a vessel carrying one of your personal stories to a new shore: college.

Right now you are writing for a college admissions audience, and that audience includes different types of people: students, alumni, and admissions counselors who work in the college's admissions office. When you are performing your story, it always helps to ask, "Who is the person am I talking to?" and "What do they need to know about me to help me connect with their college?" Students say that the more they research a specific college, the more they can create this feeling of a live performance. If you have met someone from that college—perhaps an admissions officer visited your school, or you have a neighbor or friend who went there—focus on that person. Even if you do not know anyone in particular, it helps to imagine the admissions counselor (or if you are prepping for an interview, the interviewer) very specifically. Where is the person sitting? What is he or she wearing? Why does this person work in admissions or do interviews anyway? It is likely the person works in admissions because of a belief in young people and a desire to make a difference in the lives of young people. That person wants to help you and wants to build a community. And you want to be part of that community, so give that person reasons to believe in you. But first, you need to get his or her attention.

In this chapter you are going to work closely on the beginnings and endings of your essays—the Magnet and Glow—giving you a number of different tools to make the first and last sentences more powerful and memorable. If you were working with a partner in Part 2: Shape, that person can help you work through this section too. Even better, if you can pull together a small group of people you can count on to be honest and who usually disagree about important things, then you will have a group that resembles an actual admissions committee! In the first exercise you are going to deconstruct one of your stories to identify the story's different sources of energy and emotion.

Where Is the Power?

1. Print three copies of one of your transcribed stories or essay drafts from Part 2: Shape—an essay that is still rough and needs work is great for this exercise. You will need your highlighters too, in four different colors.
2. Read through your story or essay and highlight the following:
   a. In blue highlight the main point of the essay, and label it "RTB" for "reason to believe" in you. Pick one sentence—which sentence gets closest to saying it all?
   b. In blue again, highlight all the sentences that move the action forward and label them "A" for action.
   c. In orange highlight the sentence that is emotionally the most moving to you. Again, pick just one sentence.
   d. In yellow highlight the two or three sentences that have the most memorable details.
3. Finally, in green highlight two or three sentences that need more work. Perhaps they seem confusing, or you think they are too general or things that anyone could say.

You may find yourself highlighting some sentences or parts of sentences more than once in this exercise; that is fine.

The idea of this exercise is to draw your attention to two sources of energy in your essays—the action and the details of your story. If you are like most people, you tend to place action and interpretation side by side. Your story includes a simple action, "I finished biology class and walked out into the cold." And then you tell your reader what that action means; you interpret it for them: "It was the hardest test I'd ever taken." If you are able to hold back your interpretation—which is almost always a script anyway—the reader takes the action of the story and adds the emotional resonance from his or her own memories. When you allow your reader to re-create the emotions in this way, your reader is drawn to your story and to you because that person has been able to put himself or herself into your shoes. When you do this work for the reader, telling the meaning of what you did or learned, you prevent the reader from having this empathic response. You inadvertently push the reader away.

In addition to action the other source of energy in your story comes from the three *D*'s: detail, dialogue, and description. And while your tendency is to squash action with interpretation in early essay drafts, details are almost always layered over with emotion. For example, your story ends with the following details, "I pushed past the last runner, nosed across the finish line, and looked for my grandmother in the crowd." And then you feel the need to add, "I was so proud of my victory." If you spend time exploring details, dialogue, and description—as you did in Chapter 7: Focus Out—you will have a wide variety of choices, from the story itself, to reveal your emotions to the reader. Remember: your reader is smart and experienced and knows that a victory hard earned brings a feeling of pride. So let your reader experience that pride from that person's own repository of emotions and memories. Your reader will feel—in his or her own mind and emotions—powerfully alive in your story.

Every sentence of your essay benefits from this heightened performance element: taking out the critic's vocabulary, which we have all been trained to use in most of the essays we write for school, and speaking directly, as if you are with the person. Because the first and last sentences of your essay are essential to delivering the emotional power of your story, you will practice amplifying the magnet and glow of your essay as if you are an actor on stage delivering a soliloquy in which each sentence must stand on its own merits.

Starting in the Action

Great beginnings draw people in; great endings leave them wanting to know more. Here are some intriguing beginnings I still remember, two from fiction I read long ago and one from narrative nonfiction that I read a few years back:

> "124 was spiteful." (Toni Morrison, *Beloved*)[2]
> "He was an inch, perhaps two, under six feet, powerfully built, and he advanced straight at you with a slight stoop of the shoulders, head forward, and a fixed from-under stare which made you think of a charging bull." (Joseph Conrad, *Lord Jim*)[3]
> "Six years after the fact, Dr. Paul Edward Farmer reminded me, 'We met because of a beheading.'" (Tracy Kidder, *Mountains Beyond Mountains*)[4]

Like a magnet a great beginning draws you in and makes you want more. A strong opening grabs you in one of three ways:

> It tells you something simple in a surprising or unusual way (we know what "spiteful" means, but what or who is "124"?).
> It reveals something you want to know more about (who is this character with the "stare" that makes the narrator "think of a charging bull"?).
> It presents a paradox, something that seems not to make sense at first (meeting at a "beheading").

Similar to great fiction in this respect, successful college admissions essays draw the reader in from the first sentence using action and intrigue. Great essays never begin, "This essay is going to be about. . . ." They do not restate the question—which may be a great way to get a history essay going, but is a waste of space in a personal essay. When an opening line is successful, it is almost as if the author is whispering, "Come closer, I'm going to tell you something really important." Imagine when you start your essay, you are shifting from your everyday voice to something quieter, but more powerful, and you are speaking to one person who is reading your essay and listening for your unique voice.

Let's look at where you will find the voice you want to amplify in the essay you marked up in Exercise 1: Where Is the Power?

> First, take a look at the two things you highlighted in blue—your reason to believe (RTB) and the actions that move the story forward. Are the actions and reason to believe found in the same sentence? Does the reader learn the reason to believe from the action, or is it conveyed somewhere else in the story?
> Next look at the sentences you highlighted in yellow (memorable details) and orange (most emotionally moving). Does the emotional energy of the story flow from the details—for example, "I was sweating, biting my lip, and wringing my hands"—or is emotion stated separately, outside the actions and details of the story—"I was never so scared in all my life"? What people sometimes call your topic, or theme, and we call your "reason to believe," comes through the action of the story, almost like a current that runs under the essay, something the reader experiences and figures out from reading your story. Similarly, the emotional force of the story is conveyed through the details, the way you see events and connect them for the reader.

Pivot or Persevere?

In *The Lean Startup*, Eric Ries describes the moment when a new business must decide whether to move in a new direction or add more energy to keep it moving in the same direction—the decision to "pivot" or to "persevere."[5] Students often say about their Defining Moment stories, "It was important to me, and *I know I changed*. But there wasn't really a pivot. There wasn't one moment when everything changed." If you find yourself wrestling with the structure of your story, and you are having trouble identifying the Pivot—a moment that others can experience as having changed you in some tangible way—it may help to think about the moment as one in which you chose to keep going in the same direction, but perhaps with more velocity, or knowledge, or intention. The important thing is to show your reader the actions that shaped and informed you, and what you did as a result. And if you imagine you might want to start your own business, *The Lean Startup* is a must read!

In this chapter you will learn how to drive the idea of your essay like a train on the tracks of action and detail, and you will learn how to convey the emotional underpinning of the story through those same actions and details. At this point you may be scratching your head and wondering, "If I don't tell them what I learned or what I'm feeling, how will they know?" When you construct your story so that the actions and details reveal your learning, you can trust your reader to share your experience and fill in emotions from his or her own reservoir of life experience.

The first place we are going to focus is your story's Magnet, the very first sentence. Here are some great magnets from actual student essays:

> *When I cooked with my grandmother, she used the little knife and I used the big knife.* (Zach Nicol, Northwestern University '15)
> *"I'm fine," she said, over and over.* (Liam Moore, Bucknell University '17)
> *In the maze-like middle school, my shadow was my only companion.* (Yingbin Mei, Hamilton College '16)

Each of these openings draws the reader into the story like a magnet.

> In the first example, you wonder why does the grandson use the bigger knife?
> The second example begs you to ask, "Is she really fine?"
> In the third example, why is the speaker lost in middle school?

Here are three ways to create strong Magnets:

> Put the reader in the action ("When I cooked with my grandmother . . .").
> Prompt the reader to ask, "What's next?" ("I'm fine").
> Set the scene ("the maze-like middle school").

These are not fancy openings with words plucked out of the thesaurus. They are powerful because they use common language, and they describe everyday experiences that many people can share (cooking, middle school, even the ubiquitous "I'm fine" that everyone says, but in this case appears not to be true). These Magnets are all drawn from spoken stories, so they naturally use straightforward sentence structure and vernacular language. When you are wondering how to start your story, start with action and create a picture that takes your reader to a specific place, using details from your memory and actions that unfold from your own or another person's point of view. Let's practice.

EXERCISE 2

Creating Magnets

Take the sentence you circled in orange for the most emotionally moving sentence in Exercise 1: Where Is the Power? Copy it and make it the first sentence of a new story. Remember the goal of the Magnet is to draw the reader into the actions and emotions right from the start. You are going to start with something that is already emotionally powerful and rework it using each of the following techniques for creating Magnets. For each technique, create three different Magnets.

Magnet

EXAMPLE: _My coach asked me to help our tennis team win the match._

_____

_____

Put the Reader in the Action

EXAMPLE: _We were about to lose the second set 0–6, and my coach, Arky, called me over to the fence and said, "Change something, Zach," and then he put his head down and walked away._

1. _____

_____

2. _____

_____

3. _____

_____

Prompt the Reader to Ask, "What's Next?"

EXAMPLE: _Before serving I said to my partner, "Come on. If we don't win this point, we lose game, set, match, and the team loses too."_

1. _____

_____

2. _____

_____

3. _____

_____

Set the Scene

EXAMPLE: *My hands and legs were red from the blustering wind, as the sun set behind Horace Mann.*

1. _____

   _____

2. _____

   _____

3. _____

   _____

From all nine of your examples circle the one that makes the strongest Magnet for this story. What makes it the strongest? If you like you can take this sentence, remap your story like you practiced in Chapter 8, and try performing that story again using the new Magnet as the opening sentence.

Leave Your Reader Wanting More

Just as the first sentence draws the reader into your world, the last sentence—the Glow—leaves a lasting impression that stays with the reader long after reading your essay. The Glow is the very last thing the reader will read in your essay, and often in your whole application, so you want to leave that person with something that lingers, something that connects with him or her and leaves the reader wanting to advocate for you and take action on your behalf.

Here are some great Glows from actual student essays:

> *I watched her write in big scratchy letters, "I am so happy Malore came to my house to work. Somday I want be a world changer."* (Mallory Namoff, Columbia College '17)
> *Just once I want to serenade someone with my electric violin.* (Tucker Albright, Stanford University '17)
> *Our final project turned 675 Post-Its into a mural of the Rolling Stones Tongue and Lip logo; it still hangs on my wall, a reminder of what can come of an unlikely collaboration.* (Laura Schinagle, University of Michigan '17)

Each of those sentences packs a lot of emotional power and could almost be a whole essay in itself! Once you get the hang of this, you will see—and experience when you read your own and friends' essays—that each and every sentence in your essay can deliver both action and emotion.

What makes a great ending? Just as you often need to lop off several sentences of preamble from your draft to find and then dramatize the Magnet, you may find that you need to pull back all of your final explanations and habitual closing statements to let the details and action of the Glow linger in your readers' minds. A Glow works best when it:

> Takes a surprising twist (the little girl wants to be like her mentor, Mallory)
> Leaves you wanting to know more (don't you want to hear that electric violin to find out what the author means by "serenade"?)
> Is closed but open (the completed Post-It mural embodies the possibility of "unlikely collaboration")

Here are three ways to create lasting, memorable Glows:

> Keep the reader in the action ("I watched her write. . . .").
> Leave more to be asked ("Just once. . . ." makes you wonder why does he want to serenade someone with his electric violin, and when will he get the chance?).
> Close the scene ("675 Post-Its" is the end of the action and visually memorable).

Now you will get to practice.

EXERCISE 3

Creating Glows

Take a look at the action sentences and reason to believe (RTB) you circled in blue in Exercise 1: Where Is the Power? From all of those sentences write below Glow the one sentence or idea that is the most important thing you want your reader to learn about you from this essay.

Glow

EXAMPLE: *By being a leader I helped my team overcome a tough situation.*

_____

_____

_____

Keep the Reader in the Action

EXAMPLE: *My first serve skidded in.*

1. _____

_____

2. _____

_____

3. _____

_____

Leave More to Be Asked

EXAMPLE: *Donny whispered, "Do you think we can do that again, or should we try down the middle?"*

1. _____

_____

2. _____

_____

3. _____

_____

Close the Scene

EXAMPLE: *It was past dark when the match finally ended.*

1. _____

_____

2. _____

_____

3. _____

_____

Of all your practice Glows, which one do you think will make the strongest ending for this story? Why? Working back from that Glow, remap the story and complete it as a 650-word essay.

The Rapid Revision Process

Because the first and last sentences frame your story, and have extra force as a result, we have focused on how to make your Magnet and Glow especially powerful. But these tools you have just learned to strengthen your essay's Magnet and Glow will fortify the rest of your essay too, bringing every sentence alive with your unique voice and experience.

Often when students "edit" their college application essays, they iron out the very things that make their stories powerful: the quirky voice, the idiosyncratic way of seeing things, and their mistakes and misgivings. In the rest of this chapter, you will take the essay that you marked up with highlighters and do a "rapid revision."

EXERCISE 4

Revision Decisions

If you are working with a partner, this is a great exercise to do in pairs. Give one copy of your essay to your partner, and keep one for yourself. Your partner should do the same, giving you a copy of his or her paper. Work through the essay section by section. For each section work through these questions, and fill in the chart that follows—in your book for your own essay, and in your friend's book for his or her essay. For each section of the chart consider the following:

MAGNET
1. Does the story start in the action?
2. What do you learn about the narrator from the first sentence?
3. What does the Magnet urge the reader to ask next?
4. Do you want to know more about this person?

GLOW
1. Does the essay end in the action of the story?
2. What is the thing you will remember about the person who wrote this essay?
3. Does the last sentence tie the essay up in an ending that is formulaic or predictable?
4. Can any words, phrases, or sentences be eliminated to make the glow more memorable?

DETAILS, DIALOGUE, AND DESCRIPTION

1. Are the details specific and vivid?
2. Has the author chosen details that are consistent with the action and setting of the story?
3. Are there details that seem to point in another direction, away from the story? Should they be replaced with other details? (Note: Some of the details you decide to cut may be clues to other stories.)
4. Are there any missing details—aspects of the story that need to be fleshed out a bit more for the reader?

CHARACTER

1. What do you learn about the author of this essay?
2. Are there aspects of the speaker's character that need more substance? What details or actions might reveal the missing character elements?
3. Is the speaker's tone consistent with the content of the story?
4. Would you want this person to be your roommate? Classmate? Partner for a public service project?

STRUCTURE

1. Can you identify the three beats of the story (Magnet-Pivot-Glow)? If not, what is missing?
2. Are the story elements organized in the order that is strongest emotionally? Is there another order you would suggest to heighten a different aspect of the story?
3. If two stories are combined, do they make sense together? Is the reader able to follow the jump from one story to the next? If not, what can be done to make the connection stronger?
4. Is there anything you can cut out to make the story stronger?

And then, reviewing the chart once you have completed it, what are the one or two things you want to focus on in your next round of revision?

_____

_____

_____

MAGNET

How does the first sentence draw the reader in?
What can be done to strengthen the opening?

Notes for Revision

GLOW

How does the last sentence make the emotion of the story stick with the reader?
What can be done to strengthen the ending?

Notes for Revision

THREE *D'S*

What are the most memorable details?
Where can action, external dialogue, or description replace interpretations, inner dialogue, and emotions?

Notes for Revision

CHARACTER

What do you learn about the person who wrote the essay?
What would you like to learn more about?

Notes for Revision

STRUCTURE

How can you heighten the action?
What is the strongest order for story elements?

Notes for Revision

DIRECTION

What do you want to achieve in the revision process?
Pick one or two things to focus your next revision.

Notes for Revision

Once you have reviewed your essay using the Revision Decisions chart from Exercise 4, choose one or two things to focus your next round of revision. And once that is done, your essay should be very close to finished. Be careful not to show it to too many people, as all of their well-meaning ideas may drown out your own authentic voice. And beware of over-editing, pruning and fixing, and cleaning up all the elements of your own style and voice, so the essay stops sounding like you and sounds like anyone could have written it. We will return to revisions one more time in Chapter 12: Write Out Loud. But in general college application essays are often more effective when they convey your voice of yearning and becoming, rather than someone who has everything all perfectly figured out.

The Additional Information Question

This question is optional, and you should not feel you need to put anything else here. If necessary you can use the Additional Information question to clarify other sections of the Common Application or other applications. Here are three examples that sometimes come up:

> Describe, in greater detail, any college-level courses or research you have completed while in high school. One page is usually plenty. In general, you only want to send the actual research or other assignments if the college to which you are applying specifically asks for it.

> Explain any unusual circumstances that affected your academic performance for a short period of time (an illness or family emergency or a major family move). Sometimes it is appropriate for a guidance counselor who knows you well to include this information in the letter of recommendation, so feel free to ask if your counselor is comfortable addressing any significant circumstances. But if there is not a guidance counselor who can speak to the situation, you can address it directly in your own words.

> If you attended several different high schools and your overall academic record or GPA is a composite of all of them, you may want to explain that.

You don't need to include anything that is covered elsewhere in your application. For instance, if everything on your résumé is included in the Work and Activities section of the Common App, you don't need to include your résumé. In most situations where you include Additional Information, you want to be very matter-of-fact in explaining the additional materials or circumstances. There is more information about this section in *A Guide to the New 2013–2014 Common Application (CA4)*, at the back of this book and which will be continuously updated at www.storytocollege.com/writeoutloud.

So it's fine to leave your reader asking a question or two, and definitely start and end your essay with your reader in the story's action.

Further Reading

Hallman, J.C., ed. *The Story About the Story: Great Writers Explore Great Literature.* Portland: Tin House Books, 2009.

"100 Best First Lines from Novels." Last modified 2013, www.infoplease.com/ipea/A0934311.

"The Top 10 Best Closing Lines of Novels." Last modified 2013, http://litreactor.com/columns/the-top-10-best-closing-lines-of-novels.

CHAPTER 10

Explore Perspectives

*There is nothing insignificant in the world. It
all depends on the point of view.*

—GOETHE[1]

You have probably heard more than one person say, "Your college essays need to be about you." And that is completely true. But you are also often asked to explore influences. Questions about influences come in two types: influential people and influential works of art, literature, or science.

> Describe a person who has had a significant influence on you, and how he or she has influenced you.
> Pick a character from fiction, a historical figure, or a work of art, literature, or science that has influenced you, and explain the influence.

How can you talk about these types of influences and still write essays that are fundamentally about you? How can you show that you understand and appreciate others' points of view, while revealing your own passions, hopes, and dreams? How can you bring other perspectives into your story and still maintain the power of your own stories and the integrity of your own voice? Those are the questions we will explore in this chapter.

To Be Influenced Is to Have Your Perspective Changed

The word *influence* comes from the Latin word for "flowing in." To be influenced is to be shaped or formed, by someone or something, so that it becomes a part of you. If something has an influence on you, it has power of some sort over you; it is almost as if it flows into

Words and Music

Pick a song that is important to you. How has it influenced you? Write without your pen leaving the paper or your fingers leaving the keyboard for 10 minutes or more.

you and transforms you. Our parents and teachers influence us long before we are aware of this shaping. Books, movies, television shows, and video games, as well as things in our world that we may not even pay attention to very much, such as advertising and graffiti, inform not only our ideas but also the way we think and how we respond. So an essay about an influence shows that you are aware of this process; it reveals how your beliefs have been shaped and your actions transformed by something outside of yourself—either a person or a thing.

Influences can be divided into four types: they are either people or things, and they are either living or dead (in the case of people) or they are contemporary or historical/literary (in the case of things). The chart "The Present and the Past" in Exercise 1: Influences gives you a chance to brainstorm some of your influences.

EXERCISE 1

Influences

Consider the following four categories of influence. In each of the following four boxes list at least five influences.

> Living people
> People no longer living
> Contemporary things
> Things from the past

The Present and the Past

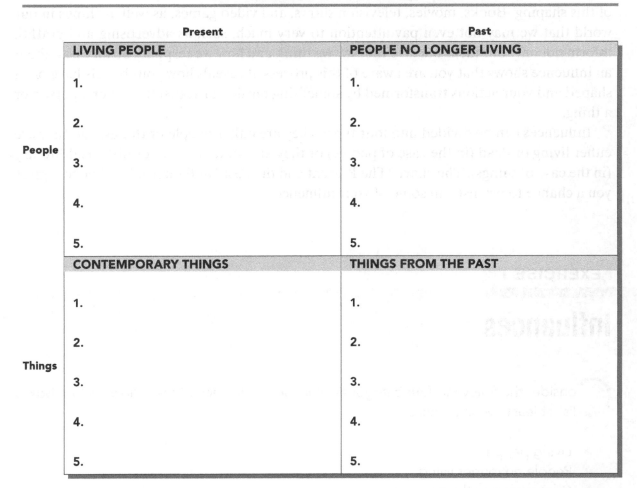

	Present	Past
People	**LIVING PEOPLE** 1. 2. 3. 4. 5.	**PEOPLE NO LONGER LIVING** 1. 2. 3. 4. 5.
Things	**CONTEMPORARY THINGS** 1. 2. 3. 4. 5.	**THINGS FROM THE PAST** 1. 2. 3. 4. 5.

Choose three items, one from each of three different boxes, and copy the influences you have chosen into the next exercise.

Moments of Influence

Step 1: List three important influences.

INFLUENCE 1	INFLUENCE 2	INFLUENCE 3

Step 2: List specific moments that demonstrate the influence.

INFLUENCE 1 MOMENTS	INFLUENCE 2 MOMENTS	INFLUENCE 3 MOMENTS

Step 3: Map a story about that influence, and write it out.

_____

_____

_____

_____

_____

_____

_____

_____

_____

_____

_____

_____

_____

_____

_____

_____

_____

_____

_____

_____

_____

_____

_____

_____

_____

Working with Family Stories

Family stories are notoriously difficult to use successfully in college application essays. Why? For many high school students, applying to college is one of the first times you have to be reflective, focusing on what has defined you in the past and articulating how you plan to define yourself and shape your world as an adult. This is an opportunity to identify some of the things you may take for granted—almost as if you are putting all of your life experiences through a sifter, letting the ones that are less important flow through, and then focusing on one significant, definitional pebble in each of your college essays. And for each of those pebbles, you are examining it from many different angles—we call these *perspectives*—until you find the ones that reveal your character to colleges.

The problem with family stories—as we explored in Chapter 3: Transform Scripts to Stories—is that they are often scripts: told over and over, almost always in the same way, becoming ossified and safe. To make stories about family members (or anyone else) work in an Influence Essay, you need to show how you have taken that person and their lessons into your own life. You make yourself the subject of an Influence Essay by showing not only how you have been influenced, but also how you shaped and transformed the people and stories that came before you to make a difference in the world.

This essay can be challenging because the people you are most likely to show your essays to—your parents or teachers—may also know the people you are writing about, and their ideas about these people may be different from yours. It is too safe and easy to write a "good little child" Influence Essay where everything is pretty and everyone behaves exactly as they should. We all know real families are not perfect. People fight; sometimes people do things that hurt other people. Sometimes our biggest influences come from watching someone make the same mistake over and over, and then choosing to act differently in our own lives. (Remember the *decision* in your own mind to act differently is not the heart of a viable essay, but a *moment when you act differently* most emphatically is.)

Sometimes we are influenced in ways that are a bit unconscious and mysterious; the Influence Essay is your chance to explore the moments when the influence happens, so others can see how you have been shaped. If you want to complete an Influence Essay about someone who is still a powerful force in your life, I recommend that you do not show your essay to that person or other people who know that person right away. This is especially true of parents, who can be tremendously valuable in many aspects of the college process but not as unbiased readers of essays about themselves! Or perhaps you want to write about a teacher you find yourself tussling with about big ideas in class; some people might even call what you do "fighting." That process of wrestling your own ideas free from a powerful influence can make a very interesting essay, more interesting oftentimes than a story line that tells a version of "This amazing person taught me a really big lesson about life." In the next exercise you are going to explore a variety of influential people and the moments that they influenced you.

Asking for Recommendations

Which Teachers Should You Ask for Letters of Recommendation?

The most valuable letters to admission officers are letters from teachers who taught you in upper level courses junior or senior year. Your junior year teachers—especially teachers in Honors, AP, or IB courses—are likely to get a lot of requests for letters of recommendation. The most important thing is letters of recommendation from two teachers of academic subjects in which you have performed strongly.

What If I Don't Have Two Teachers Who Know Me That Well?

Can I ask a coach, a club advisor, or someone else who knows me better? Usually a letter from a coach, advisor, or someone who was your supervisor at work would be used as a third letter, not one of your two main academic references. Ask your teachers first.

How Should I Ask Them?

Ideally, you have spent time getting to know this teacher; you have performed well and you have gone beyond the basic requirements of the course. The teacher has seen evidence of your intellectual commitment and creativity. Schedule an appointment with the teacher, to make sure that the time is available and you can prepare for the meeting. Some students find it helpful to type up a short list of talking points to help the teacher remember their accomplishments in the course, and they bring those lists to their meetings.

When you ask for a recommendation, try something along these lines in your own words, "Mrs. Bressler, I am applying to 10 colleges in the fall, and your class is one that has really influenced my choices. I was wondering if you would consider writing a letter of recommendation for my applications?" Listen to what your teacher has to say. If for any reason your teacher has reservations or prefers not to write a letter, thank the teacher and look for someone else. If the teacher says yes, offer the list of things you accomplished in that teacher's course as a reminder and say, "I really appreciate this, and I know you have a lot of these letters to write, so I typed up a list of things I am most proud of about your course." Even if the teacher gives you an enthusiastic yes, I would ask, "Is there anything that you see I could have done better in your class to prepare for college, or anything else I can learn that you haven't already told me?" This will give you great information about what you need to work on in the future and may also suggest to you places where the teacher is a bit uncertain about your record.

Influential People

FAMILY MEMBER

What They Said

What They Did

A Moment That Shows Their Influence on You

PEER OR COMMUNITY MEMBER

What They Said

What They Did

A Moment That Shows Their Influence on You

What They Said

What They Did

A Moment That Shows Their Influence on You

As you complete your Influence Essay, bring that person to life through a story. Imagine for the time that person shows up in your essay you are performing with that person's voice and mannerisms. Here are some more tips for writing about influential people:

> Dialogue is a great tool to bring essays about people to life (see Chapter 7: Focus Out for how to use quotations in your writing).
> Consider writing about a person you do not know but think about frequently, or someone who is no longer living but who influences you as much as a living person (or more).
> It is easy for Influence Essays to get vague and general. Demonstrate the character's influence on you by showing the character and/or yourself in action.
> Avoid these clichés and filler: *It transformed me*; *I wasn't the same*; *important*; *impact*; and *role model*.

For many students it can be even more challenging to write about influential works of art, literature, or science than about living people because most of your previous writing about those topics has been critical essays assigned in school. If a college gives you the option to submit an essay that you have completed in school, you should definitely send (or upload) one that is your best work and includes your teacher's comments. In fact, the more teacher comments the better, so the college gets a sense of what your school is like. But you should not answer a question about an influential work of art, literature, history, or science by submitting a critical essay instead of writing a personal essay about the influence. The Influence Essay—whether about a person who is living or someone who is fictional or dead; something animate or inanimate—is an opportunity to reveal how your ideas have been shaped, and what actions you have taken as a result. In the next exercise, you will explore literary and historical influences as if they are living people, since the idea of a successful Influence Essay is to bring your influence to life.

EXERCISE 4

Influential Works of Art, Literature, and Science

HISTORICAL FIGURE

What They Said or Did

Sensory Details

A Moment That Shows Their Influence on You

FICTIONAL CHARACTER

What They Said or Did

Sensory Details

A Moment That Shows Their Influence on You

CREATIVE WORK

What They Said or Did

Sensory Details

A Moment That Shows Their Influence on You

Here are some tips for bringing an essay about the influence of art, literature, or science to life for your reader:

> If you have a copy of the work in front of you—a copy of the book or a postcard of the painting you are discussing—you will be able to find specific examples more easily.

> This essay should *not* be written as art, literature, or historical criticism. The question asks how the work has influenced you, not what you think about it.

> Stuck for ideas? Take a couple hours and visit a local sculpture garden, museum, or library.

> This essay is a great opportunity to write about something you studied outside of school.

> I often get asked if it is OK to write about contemporary art, television, or video games. The answer is definitely yes—write about something you know really well that has shaped you in some important and lasting way.

> Avoid these clichés and filler: *I was moved*; *I was inspired*; *it was powerful*; and *it came alive*.

Exploring Perspectives

On stage each person inhabits a unique perspective that is his or her character's way of being in the world.[2] One of the skills that leads to college success is the ability to experience the world from multiple perspectives, to be open to all the different points of view that students and faculty bring from their very different life experiences. One of the most powerful ways to shape the Influence Essay—and one that we will explore further in the following exercise—is to bring another perspective to life in your essay. It is almost as if more than one perspective resides in your essay; you are able to show that your own thoughts and actions include the knowledge and experience of others. College includes many opportunities for working with multiple perspectives—everything from figuring out who will get the top bunk and how to negotiate different sleep schedules, to classes that explore contested contemporary issues from various points of view.

How to Approach Supplements

I encourage you to think of each supplement question as an opportunity to show colleges another part of your character, to add another chapter to the story you create for the admissions officer who reads your application as a whole. Whenever possible, you should treat each "optional" essay on the college's supplement as another chance to speak directly with the college admissions officer and show that person something important about your character and ambitions.

After completing *Write Out Loud* you will have a portfolio of stories of the types you will need to answer each college's supplement questions:

Defining Moments
Community
Influences
Issues
Activities
Why I Have Chosen This Major
Why I Want to Attend This College

If a college asks a different question, you can almost always go back into your Story Portfolio and find a Defining Moment from your past that reveals an answer to the question in the present.

And here is a bit of strategy to wrestle all those supplements into shape:

1. First, make a chart of all the supplement essays you need to complete.
2. For each type of essay, write the longest version of each essay first. For instance, perhaps you need to write three different essays about community, and they are 150, 200, and 400 words long. Write the one that is 400 words long first, using a three-sentence story to organize it. Then you can prune the longer essay into shorter versions—as many times as you need—maintaining the story's integrity and forward motion by keeping that solid three-sentence story structure.
3. Finally, for each supplement for each college, you want to make a specific connection with that college. Remember to replace all general statements like, "I've always wanted to go to college in the city," with specific details such as "I am attracted to Houston because. . . ." Remember those notes you took while visiting colleges—about the classes you sat in on, the person who interviewed you, and that great Ethiopian restaurant on College Avenue? You can use all those memories to spice up your Why This College question. Make sure to double-check your facts. For instance, if you are writing about your intended college major, use *exactly* the name the college uses for that major, and take the time to look through the classes and speak specifically about which ones you want to take.

Connect with Your Colleges

Most students spend hours and hours on their personal essays for the Common Application, polishing them again and again, but save their supplements for the last minute. This is a big mistake!

Each college asks its own supplement questions; your answers help the college determine whether you will be a good fit for its unique programs and community.

Use the two charts on the following pages to help you keep track of the details of each college community so you can make specific connections to each college in your supplement essays. You can also download these charts at www.storytocollege.com/writeoutloud.

Know Your Colleges

Get to know the colleges you are applying to. Do your research and use the following Know Your Colleges chart to organize the information that you find. Think about which classes you would take, what clubs you would participate in, and how you would add to their community.

Know Your Community

Reflect on the communities that you are already a part of. Use the Know Your Community chart to organize all of your information. Connect the things you want to do at that college with activities you've already done. The time you take to make these connections for each college will not only help you get in but also help you hit the ground running once you arrive!

HIGH SCHOOL CLASS SIZE   Think about your high school. How did its size and learning environment influence your learning? Do you want to know all your classmates by name? Will you succeed better in small, discussion-based classes or large lectures?

DESCRIBE YOUR COMMUNITIES   Each person is a member of multiple communities. Think about the different communities you belong to (school, religious, family, etc.). List all the communities that you contribute to and how you contribute.

RESEARCH INTERESTS + EXPERIENCES   Many colleges provide opportunities for students to conduct research. What are you interested in researching? What type of research have you already done (this can be independent research, work you've done with a teacher, or something as simple as scouring YouTube videos to come up with your own acne cure)?

TRAVEL INTERESTS + EXPERIENCES   Many colleges provide study abroad opportunities. What places have you traveled to already? What were your key experiences there? How did you contribute to those communities? Where are you interested in going? How will you contribute to the communities to which you travel in the future? What are you hoping to learn from your travels?

COMMUNITY PROFILE   What is the makeup of your current community? Where are people from? How do they interact? What issues affect your community? What are the accomplishments of your community? How will your experiences and interactions add value to the specific college communities you are applying to? What perspective will you bring? What issues are you committed to?

SUBJECTS THAT INTERESTED YOU IN HIGH SCHOOL   What subjects interested you in high school? What did you do outside of school to pursue those interests? How does each specific college you are applying to provide an opportunity to expand that interest?

Know Your Colleges

College Name	Class Size	Location	Research Opportunities	Study Abroad Opportunities	Class Profile
Example: Dartmouth	1,098	Rural: Hanover, NH	First Year Summer Research Opportunity	45 programs with a 61% participation rate. #1 in Ivy League.	10% first-generation college students.

Major	Courses	Professors	Sports	Clubs	How You Connect
Economics	Economics in Developing Countries	David Blanchflower: research interests include wage determination, happiness, self-employment, and unions. Published "Young people and the recession."	28 club sport teams with 75% of student body participating.	Environmental Conservation Organization	I left Ghana when I was 10 years old to come to the U.S. I would be the first in my family to go to college. I want to gain the necessary skills to help Ghana's economy thrive. I think Dartmouth's study abroad program and economics courses could help me achieve this goal.

Know Your Community

High School Class Size	Describe Your Communities	Research Interests + Experiences	Travel Interests + Experiences	Community Profile

Subjects That Interested You in High School	Courses That Inspired You in High School	Sports	Activities	What Do You Add to Your Community?

COURSES THAT INSPIRED YOU IN HIGH SCHOOL   What courses inspired or motivated you to reach new goals? Was there a specific project, teacher, or field trip that transformed your perspective? How will you continue to achieve your goals and commitments at each of the colleges you are applying to?

SPORTS   What sports do you participate in? How does playing sports reveal your character? What would you contribute to the sports community at the specific schools you are applying to?

ACTIVITIES   What activities do you participate in? Do you participate in them in school or outside of school? Why are these activities important to you? How would you continue to pursue these activities or other activities at the colleges you are applying to?

WHAT DO YOU ADD TO YOUR COMMUNITY?   Think about all the ways you contribute to your own communities. What does your unique character and perspective add to those communities? What do you bring from your personal experiences to the specific colleges you are applying to?

EXERCISE 5

Looking from the Other Perspective

Pick one of your influences from Exercise 1: Influences, earlier in this chapter, and give the name.

INFLUENCE: _____

Free write 800 words as if you are that person. Look at the world from your influence's point of view. What does your influence see? What does your influence do? Whom does your influence know? What does your influence say when he or she sees you watching?

_____

_____

_____

_____

_____

What was it like to write from another point of view? Perhaps you can use some of the details from that exploration in your Influence Essay.

The following essay flows back and forth between the student's perspective and the experience and energy of **Paul Lee**, a community organizer in Chinatown.

"Vote for Paul Lee for District Leader!" My face brightened as morning commuters passed by and took flyers from my hand. As they turned the corner, they carelessly tossed the flyers away. My brows furrowed. Is this what I woke up at seven in the morning for? To hand out flyers to indifferent strangers who won't give the time of day, nevertheless a second glance? I was just a background character, a boy handing out flyers in the scene of a lively street. I was a mannequin, easily passed by unnoticed.

After my flyer shift had ended, my boss took me out to lunch at a diner. My eyes were darting back and forth, unsure of the situation. My boss slouched casually in his seat across from me. I had only met him twice before and instinctively, I began surreptitiously examining him. I slyly lowered my menu and peered over the "wall." He wore a simple white polo shirt, and his greying hair was brushed back in an old 1960s hairstyle. He seemed like just an average Chinese man. The waiter came and pulled me out of my idle thoughts. As we made our orders, he put down his menu, and said, "How about a story?"

He opened with a story about his stint with the army, when he brashly enlisted at the Chinatown recruitment center. Next was a lighthearted tale of his moment of "stardom" when he debuted on the silver screen in Hollywood. Finally, the curtains closed with a story of an "extreme makeover" of his parents' antique store to a game shop.

I vicariously experienced the vivid fragments of his past through his stories. I felt the hope and energy of a young man slightly short in stature, but big in heart, enlisting in the army, the excitement of a risk taker trying to make it big in Hollywood, and the freedom of a high spirited man who followed his hobby and turned his parents' antique store to a game shop.

In my mind Paul Lee had transcended the typical mannequin of an average Chinese man. I had inadvertently made the same oversight as the people that passed me on the street. I fit him into a general mold without trying to see him as an individual, just as they did to me. Looking around me, I had been blind. Every person in the room had a unique story and character just like Paul had his, and I had mine.

Upon my realization, I found the courage to convey my own unique character to Paul through my ideas. There is a balance between practicality, creativity, and fun that I have come to hold at the highest value in my life. I proposed to Paul an idea that was the embodiment of the three—to host carnival games at the Pavilion with a voter registration stand on the side. Instead of discarding my idea as I had expected, Paul encouraged it.

Throughout the next week, the volunteers worked to create flyers, brainstorm ideas for games, and gather prizes. However, on the day it all came together, it rained. Discouraged, I looked to Paul only to see that he was still in high spirits. In that moment I knew I couldn't be the same defeated, overlooked mannequin handing out fliers in the street. Optimism and vitality surged through the mannequin within me. I wiped the scowl from my face and proudly presented to him the six registration forms we received that day with a smile. The mannequin had come to life; I was no longer a background character but the center of the scene.

—KENNETH LEE (Cornell University '17)

Although this essay includes a number of thoughts and interpretations, the presence of Paul Lee as a character brings the story of influence to life.

Here is another Influence Essay that started out as a very predictable essay about "how Hawthorne influenced me," but when Michael took on Hawthorne's perspective it not only opened up what she could say (because he could say things she could not), but also her ability to show the power of Hawthorne's influence by inhabiting his point of view right from the start of the essay.

There was a girl and her name was Michael. This girl first picked up a camera when she was seven. It was a point-and-shoot camera, but it was hers. The upgraded camera she got for her 15th birthday was hers also. And so was my book. One summer she was in Florida. Her hair was dripping from the pool water, her skin shimmered in the blazing sunlight, and her eyes squinted at her stack of books. She picked the smallest of the bunch; she picked mine. The one labeled "Hawthorne." It only had one story and she read it quickly. "Hm," she said as she finished the first time. She said, "What?" when she finished the second time, and at the third ending she raised her sunglasses over her head and squinted at the sun. "Beautiful," she murmured. She grabbed a pencil and wrote "There is no absolute beauty. There is only what you make of it" on the last page of my story.

Back home she was entering another photo contest. This one had a theme of beauty. She booked the studio for two hours and brought in her friend. Her friend had high cheek bones, emerald eyes, curly red hair, and lips that sat outward. She was short but had the body of a dancer. When she moved everyone watched, mouths slightly ajar. Her muscles flexed and released with ease. Michael placed the girl in a wooden chair, turned her face upward toward the enormous lights and took a photo of every angle she could possibly get. She switched from black and white to high resolution, back to black and white. When the photos developed she never picked the winning shot for herself. "This is the one," said her teacher.

"Wow, you don't need to take any more pictures, Michael, this is it," said her peers. Michael went home that night and gazed at the photo. Her brow wrinkled and eyes narrowed. She put the photo in her drawer and went to sleep. The next day Michael set out with her most basic camera, the one that is always on her person. She's walking up 34th street and sees a woman. This woman had dirty skin and dirty clothes. Her blackened flingers held a sign that said "I'm hungry." Her eyes were vacant, and she looked to the side. Her eyes were trained in that direction and never moved. Michael took out her camera and took a quick picture, just one. She went to develop it that same day and put it in a folder to take home. On her bed, cross-legged, she sat looking at the red-haired girl. Her eyes cast upward, her cheek bones highlighted; Michael's mom gazed at the picture and said, "That should be in *Vogue*." Michael pulled out the other picture, of the hungry woman and placed it next to the other. Her eyes widened as she saw how the light created a shadow over the woman's face. There was no dirt, just an eye looking away. "Now that," her mother said, "shouldn't be. Easy choice, huh?"

"Yes, it is," Michael said. She placed her finger over the shadow and tapped the photo four times. She smiled. She folded the color image in half and put it in her drawer; she placed the photo of the woman in a protective folder and placed it in her bag. As she laid down that night she smirked into the glow of the TV. She said, "There is no beauty. There is only what we make of it," and closed her eyes.

—MICHAEL SHEFFEY (Howard University '16)

Two People, One Story

Now I invite you to try juxtaposing two perspectives into one Influence Essay. You have two stories: one from your influence's perspective and one from your own perspective showing what you did as a result of the influence. Write each of those stories out as a three-sentence story here:

Story from Influence's Perspective

Magnet: _____

_____

Pivot: _____

_____

Glow: _____

_____

Story About Influence from My Perspective

Magnet: _____

_____

Pivot: _____

_____

Glow: _____

_____

In the next exercise, you will use the Defining Moment Map to combine the two stories into one story with three beats, a combined Magnet-Pivot-Glow.

Two Perspectives, One Defining Moment Map

Use the Defining Moment Map to shape the two perspectives into one story.

MAGNET

⬇

PIVOT

⬇

GLOW

THEMES/IDEAS TO EXPLORE FURTHER

Framing

Here is another way you can explore perspectives in a college application essay. Imagine that each person in every essay is a character on stage. If anyone moves, all the perspectives shift. Every moment in your life is like that—one person's choices and actions affect everyone else; when one person shifts, everyone shifts. Whenever you introduce another person, another perspective, or even a new story into your essay, you give yourself the opportunity to introduce many new ideas. You can shift the frame of reference between the characters and explore the moment from different points of view. The next exercise allows you to give it a try.

EXERCISE 8

Shifting the Frame

First of all, you need a frame. You can pick up an inexpensive cardboard frame for a couple dollars from an art supply store, or you can make one from a recycled piece of cardboard. Your frame does not need to be fancy, but you want the hole in the middle of the frame to be at least 5 × 7 inches.

Take your frame and go for a walk for at least 20 minutes. Go to a few different places—common, everyday places you walk through frequently—as if you are on a journey, and each place you stop is a different station. At each station you visit, and as you walk between different stations, hold the frame up to your face, move it back and forth, and notice how the frame of reference shifts. What happens when you look at everyday objects up close and far away? What happens when you look at people from different angles and directions? Perhaps you want to look at yourself in the mirror, and move the frame forward and back, as if you are another character in your story.

Any method that you use the frame to explore perspectives is fine. You can write down ideas as you go through this journey, or when you are done, whichever you prefer.

_____

_____

_____

_____

_____

_____

Notice how you can bring different parts of the picture up close, or move them back into the distance, simply by shifting your perspective. Similarly, even when different people are part of the same experience, their stories and their perspectives are different. In your college essays, you want to heighten your unique perspective (one of the three things that colleges are looking for in your application) and show that you are able to see your perspective in relation to other people with different, sometimes even conflicting, perspectives.

Finally, you can think of each of your college applications as a frame through which that college sees you. Are there parts of your picture that you want to emphasize for different colleges? What is the most important aspect of your character for each college to know? Make sure those details are included in your essays and interview for that college.

Further Reading

Allain, Paul. *The Art of Stillness: The Theatre Practice of Tadashi Suzuki*. New York: Palgrave Macmillan, 2003.

Bonney, Jo, ed. *Extreme Exposure: An Anthology of Solo Performance Texts from the Twentieth Century*. New York: Theatre Communications Group, 2000.

CHAPTER 11

Raise the Stakes

The self is not something ready-made, but something in continuous formation through choice of action.

—JOHN DEWEY[1]

Students often describe feeling like their essays don't "matter enough." There are many ways this feeling emerges in the questions students ask in the process of completing and preparing to send their essays to colleges.

At the heart of this cry—"my essay doesn't matter enough"—is a fear that we all experience sometimes: that we are not good enough, that who we really are and what we have really experienced is somehow not adequate—for college, for work, for whatever. This fear about one's own limitations often arises close to the end of the process. You are finishing your essays, and one day you feel great about them, and the next day you feel like you want to flush them all down the toilet and not apply to college at all. As I approach the end of *Write Out Loud*, my third book, that feeling comes and goes several times each day.

If you feel "my essay doesn't matter enough," you should Refresh and let that thought go, with a gentle reminder that you and your essays are perfect, just as they are and just as you are. But there is another side to this cry that I want you to take seriously, for there is always more we can do, or a different way we can be in the world to secure the future—and the present—for all people. So for now, and the space of this chapter, I encourage you to let your essays be whole, as they are, while you also consider ways to position your stories and your life in ways that are more substantial and meaningful.

Identify Issues Important to You

What does it mean to raise the stakes of your college application essays? Take some time in Exercise 1: Raise the Stakes to answer that question for yourself.

REFRESH

You Are the President

You have just been elected President of the United States (or leader of your country). What are you going to do on your first day on the job? Write without your pen leaving the paper or your fingers leaving the keyboard for 10 minutes or more.

Raise the Stakes

Make a list of 10 ways you could raise the stakes in your college application essays and your life right now.

1._____

2._____

3._____

4._____

5._____

6._____

7._____

8._____

9._____

10._____

When I ask students in Story To College courses what it means to raise the stakes in their college application essays, here are some of their answers:

> I would have to do something that matters . . . today.
> There are lots of places I can make a difference.
> I know what I should do. I need to do it.
> Honestly I really don't want to leave my little bubble; I just want them to admit me.
> I'm just one person, what can I really do?

The phrase "raise the stakes"—or "up the ante"—comes from poker. To "raise the stakes" is to put more money on the table, to risk more for a potentially bigger reward. That's why people often resist. It may feel a bit uncomfortable, even risky, to try new things, or to respond to everyday things, or even to write about things in ways that are different and new.

The next exercise is an opportunity to explore just where your own stakes lie, the places in your life where you are genuinely committed to issues bigger than you can solve yourself. This exercise requires a few other people, so invite your friends and call it a party!

EXERCISE 2

Issues Wall

This exercise works really well with a group of six to eight people and a wall where you can post things—either with thumbtacks or masking tape. For each person you will need seven 4" × 6" index cards (preferably in bright colors) and a permanent marker. Select someone who will be the group's facilitator (making sure the work gets done) and someone else to be the scribe (the person who documents the process and shares it with the group).

1. The facilitator gives each person seven brightly colored index cards and a marker.
2. Each person writes *one* issue that is important to that person on each of three different index cards.
3. One by one, when ready, each person goes to the wall and tapes the cards to the wall, looks out at the group, and states his or her three issues. Example: *I go to the wall; tape my lemon, lime, and orange colored index cards to the wall; look out at the group; and say, "Education access. Gay marriage. Prosperity for all people."*
4. Once everyone has added his or her issues to the wall, all the participants take another three index cards and write down moments when each of their issues became important to them.

5. This round, people add just one issue at a time to the wall. You look at the group and read from the card, or tell it as a story, and then tape or tack the card with the story on top of the card that names that issue. Example: *I read from my magenta card, "My great-grandfather Emmanuel pulled my grandmother out of school when she was 12 to start cleaning houses. When I was in college she wrote me letters almost every day that had no grammar or punctuation. She just wrote one long sentence about everything she did until she ran out of paper and signed it, 'Love, Nana.' I always wondered what she would have done if she had been able to finish school." And then I tape the magenta card on top of the one that says "Education access."*

6. Go around the group until everyone has read the stories about how each of their issues became important to them.

7. On your last index card choose the issue that is most important to you right now, and write your name and "I commit to making a difference around [NAME OF ISSUE] by . . ." and complete the sentence with something specific you will do in the present around that issue.

8. Each person goes to the wall one last time, reads from the index card, and then places it on top of the story that goes with that issue. Example: *I go to the wall and read "Carol Barash. I commit to making a difference around education access by teaching high school students how to take control of the college admissions process through personal storytelling," and then I put that card on top of my grandmother's story.*

9. The scribe takes a picture of the wall with a cell phone, collects the cards, types up all the stories and commitments, and shares them with the group and—if the group agrees—with Story To College.

If you choose to do the exercise by yourself, share your final story and commitment with at least one person a day for the next three days.

So now you have an issue, and you have the beginning of a story about how that issue has meaning in your own life experience. The next step is to take that issue and write about it in a way that is meaningful to other people—even people who may disagree with you about the issue, and about what you want to do to make a difference. As I am finishing the revisions of this book, I keep clicking on the video of Gabby Giffords talking at the Senate hearing about gun control.[2] It is very hard not to be moved by her story and her experience. When you put yourself and your experience into an issue, you instantly raise the stakes and people need to take you seriously. They may not agree with you, but they are likely to respect your passion, commitment, and willingness to be vulnerable in the service of others. Getting to that place and feeling powerful about the origins of your own commitments is at the core of the work you will do in this chapter. In Exercise 3: Perspectives on Your Issue you will use the skills you learned in Chapter 10: Explore Perspectives, and explore different ways of looking at and talking about the issue where you just made a commitment to make a difference!

Perspectives on Your Issue

You are going to work as a reporter to research three different perspectives on your issue: a subject matter expert, someone who has been personally affected by the issue, and someone who is working to make a change around this issue. For each person write out at least five things that person might say to a reporter about the issue.

Subject Matter Expert

Use the Internet to identify a scholar or author who has researched and written about facts related to the issue. Include that person's name and where you completed your research, plus five facts you learned from his or her work:

Name of Expert: _____

Publication: _____

FIVE FACTS

1. _____

2. _____

3. _____

4. _____

5. _____

Person Affected

This could be you, someone you know, or someone else who has been personally affected in some way by the issue. List the person's name, how he or she was affected, and at least five ways the person has been affected in his or her own words.

Name of Person Affected: _____

How They Were Affected: _____

FIVE QUOTATIONS (in the person's exact words)

1. _____

2. _____

3. _____

4. _____

5. _____

Activist

This is someone working to make some sort of change around this issue. Include the person's name, the name of his or her organization, the organization's mission or vision, and five things the person is doing to make a change in the present.

Name of Activist: _____

Organization's Name: _____

Organization's Mission: _____

FIVE SPECIFIC ACTIONS

1. _____

2. _____

3. _____

4. _____

5. _____

After completing this exercise, you should have many more specific facts and details about your issue, as well as three different ways to approach any issue: research, experience, and action. You can use these details to develop your response to the Issue Essay—any version of "Describe an issue that has affected you, and what you are doing to make a difference around that issue." A word of caution: many students use the Issue Essay as an opportunity to go back into their critical essay voice and write as if they are the experts, giving a lecture and telling other people what they should do. If you have given public talks about your issue, that is great. And if your talks are videotaped, you may want to upload some clips to YouTube and include a link to one of them in your applications.

The Portfolio Model

Higher education is undergoing an upheaval from within. As recently as 50 years ago, if you graduated from college in the United States you were pretty much guaranteed a good-paying job for as long as you wanted to work. While a college degree is still a crucial indicator of lifetime job opportunities, a college degree is no longer enough to ensure work or economic success. Further complicating your decision, three parts of college that used to be tied together in your degree program are now separate skill sets that you are on your own to piece together from a variety of college and other courses and experiences.

For high school students attending college in the twenty-first century, to gain employment and succeed professionally, you will need to produce—and continuously expand—your portfolio in three critical areas: subject matter expertise, training and certifications, and skills for community-building, collaboration, and cocreation.

Subject Matter Expertise

What are the areas of knowledge that you want to know at a world-class level, either by studying the information yourself or serving as a uniquely valuable "curator" of other people's expertise? You can think of your college major as a potential area to gain subject matter expertise (SME). An activity that you run and where you engage with other leaders—both on campus and especially in the broader community—is another area where you will gain subject matter expertise. Since there is so much information available through the Internet, it is increasingly important that whatever other knowledge you gain in college you acquire the skills to (1) sort through all of that information, (2) sift what is fact from what is opinion or myth, and (3) identify the key issues, metrics, and the most important thought leaders in the subject.

Training and Certifications

This is an area that is shifting quite rapidly. Even 10 years ago a degree in engineering from a top Engineering program would guarantee you a job as an engineer. But something quite revolutionary is bubbling up through massive open online courses (MOOCs) and other online training programs. There are core competencies in many fields that you can now study—for free or nearly free—from the top professors at the top universities. Take a look at everything that is offered on Coursera (www.coursera.com) and Udacity (www.udacity.com). You can even take these courses in high school. And some of them allow you to receive certificates of completion and competency for a lot less than the price of taking that same course on a college campus. So it is important to identify what are the essential training and certifications required for your chosen profession, and then to make sure you achieve them—either in college or by some other path.

Community, Collaboration, and Cocreation

Back in the twentieth-century university, broadly speaking, most people received subject matter expertise in their majors, and the training and certifications for a specific type of job were conferred with their college degrees. Along with the knowledge and skills to enter a profession (or a graduate school that would start you further up the ladder in that same profession), college provided a core sense of identity and community for many people. College taught—and still teaches—students how to live in a community and how to lead that community by allowing them opportunities to run projects with small groups of people.

Technology has separated this essential, social-emotional component of college learning from the part of college that involves training and certification in various job-related skills. And the widening gap between who can afford to attend a selective college and who cannot makes it less and less likely that this core community-building function of college will survive the current upheavals in higher education. If you are planning not merely to survive, but to thrive and lead in the twenty-first century, you will want to participate in the most robust educational communities and networks possible, and you should plan to continue nurturing and growing those networks for the rest of your life.

In the twenty-first century, your calling card will be a combination of your access to subject matter expertise; your skills, training, and certifications to complete the work at hand; and your ability to collaborate and lead diverse global communities in continuous invention and reinvention of learning and life.[3] And when you need to build a bridge to that new place, remember your storytelling tool kit and start building your new community based on where you've been and where you want to go in the future.

Here are some tips about how to use facts and figures, and some other suggestions to writing an Issue Essay that is moving to all members of the audience, not just the ones who agree with you already:

> When you include facts or figures, quickly cite where you found your information. Wikipedia, your friend's blog, and the *Congressional Record* are very different information sources!

> It is often helpful to include one or two facts about the issue, but remember people are much more apt to remember stories than facts, so get to the story efficiently, rather than getting bogged down in facts.[4]

> Avoid these clichés and filler: *passionate, committed, realized, important, transformational, meaningful*, and *make a difference.*

> It is very powerful to connect the issue to your own experience—both how the issue has affected you and what you have done in the world as a result.

> Use one of your stories to show the impact the issue has had on your life.

> Consider the challenges the issue raises when you look at it from local, national, and global perspectives.

Where have you made an impact? Where do you want to make an impact? The next two exercises will help you to explore and frame your issue from three different perspectives, and especially from your own.

Framing the Issue

This exercise gives you the chance to brainstorm the importance of three different issues, each from the perspective of your local community, your country, and the world. Pick three issues, and consider each of them from these three different vantage points.

Issue Brainstorm Chart

Issue 1:
As a Local Issue
As a National Issue
As a Global Issue

Issue 2:

As a Local Issue

As a National Issue

As a Global Issue

Issue 3:

As a Local Issue

As a National Issue

As a Global Issue

The next exercise allows you to explore three different issues in relation to your own life.

EXERCISE 5

Issues and Experiences

Choose three issues that are important to you, and explore three moments when each of them has intersected with your life experience. Feel free to use issues you chose in Exercise 1: Raise the Stakes or Exercise 4: Framing the Issue, earlier in this chapter, or different ones, using this exercise as an opportunity to explore how a wide variety of issues are threads woven into your life, perhaps subtly and in the background.

Issue *LGBT rights*

1. *My friend Rachel said, "I kissed Susannah last night. I mean I really kissed her."*

2. _____

3. _____

Issue 1 _____

1. _____

2. _____

3. _____

Issue 2 _____

1. _____

2. _____

3. _____

Issue 3

1. _____

2. _____

3. _____

Choose the moment that best reveals an issue you will be involved with in college, and write a three-sentence story about that moment:

_____

_____

_____

_____

_____

_____

_____

_____

_____

_____

_____

_____

_____

_____

_____

_____

_____

_____

Next, you will focus on your unique perspective on one issue—the intersection of that issue and your own experience—and then you will map and draft your Issue Essay.

Issue of Importance

From the work you have done in the last round of exercises, what is the issue you can most imagine yourself getting involved with in college and after college? What is your personal experience and what unique perspective do you have on that issue? Which moments reveal that perspective to your audience?

Issue: A Problem or Topic That Matters to You

_____

_____

Perspective: Your Point of View

_____

_____

Moments That Show Issue Is Important to You

_____

_____

_____

_____

_____

_____

_____

Issues Map

Use the Defining Moment Map to map your Issue Essay.

MAGNET

⬇

PIVOT

⬇

GLOW

THEMES/IDEAS TO EXPLORE FURTHER

Here is an Issue Essay that flows from that last exercise:

> The blazing heat and salt-filled air surround me as I guide Samir and his family to the shiny device waiting for them near my aunt's van. The device is a solar cooker. Samir asks in broken English, "What does the propane go?"
>
> "No propane. It doesn't need propane. It cooks from the sun." He stares back at me with a look of amazement.
>
> It was the summer of 2011, during my third trip to the fishing villages of Pamban Island, off the coast of southern India. Since 2009, I have been visiting these villages to help the people there through various means: from bringing laptops to educate teenagers in basic computer skills, to raising money to buy backpacks for more than a hundred schoolchildren. Based on my previous work on the island, my school awarded me a grant to bring solar cookers to the villagers on Pamban Island. There are around 42 villages on Pamban Island, and I have already installed cookers in 5 of them, just 37 more to go!
>
> —MICHAEL DAS (University of Illinois '17)

When you take the time to explore issues from different perspectives, your life immediately exists on a bigger stage simply by seeing all the ways that issues intersect with your life but often go unrecognized: a conversation with a friend, a leak in the basement after a big storm, your mother speaking English but not writing it. And the actions that you take today—what if everyone took the same action you choose to take? What if no one did? What can you do to show why others should get involved and take action as you have chosen to do?

Another way to raise the stakes is by accessing and emboldening the community to achieve your goals. When you tell a story about how an issue became important to you—so important that you did something—you encourage others to take action as well. When this spirit of commitment and bold leadership comes through in your essays, you are much more likely to be admitted to selective colleges. But that is the least of it. You will be out in the world doing work that matters to yourself and other people. The impact and rewards of those actions stretch further and grow deeper than just getting into college; they create who you are in the world.

Should I Send Anything Else?

In college admissions less is more. You want to convey the essentials, a snapshot of what you have done and what you plan to do in college and beyond college, in the smallest number of pages possible (think *Dubliners*, not *Ulysses*). You only want to send colleges material that is relevant to who you will be in college.

> > That history research paper you worked on for more than a month? Only send it if (1) the college asks for a research paper (in which case send it with your teacher's comments), or (2) it is college-level research that you plan to continue in college.

> What about an additional letter of recommendation from your father's boss who is an alumnus of the college? Unless you worked for the person, and he or she can speak specifically to the kind of work you will do in college, probably not.

There are two areas where students usually send additional material: athletics and arts, both of which have separate requirements.

Sports

If you are not planning to continue as a varsity athlete in college, you do not need to submit any additional material about your high school athletic career with your college applications. Even if you were the captain of three high school sports teams, just list those as activities, and that is enough. On the other hand, if you want to play varsity athletics at the university level, there are strict NCAA guidelines you must follow. In addition to the following basic information, make sure to speak with your coach and guidance counselor for the specific rules that apply to your sport and the division(s) to which you are applying.

The best place to find information and guidelines governing collegiate athletics is the NCAA Eligibility Center: www.ncaapublications.com/productdownloads/CBSA.pdf is a step-by-step guide to the recruitment process and www.ncaa.org/wps/wcm/connect/public/NCAA/Eligibility/Becoming+Eligible/Recruiting focuses on eligibility.

GENERAL OUTLINE OF PROCESS

> High school athlete connects with college coaches (you may initiate contact, but your coach cannot contact them, and they cannot contact you outside of the NCAA Guidelines).
> Coaches visit students and their schools and watch them compete.
> Quiet Period: No face-to-face contact is allowed.
> Dead Period: No contact is allowed except through letters and e-mail.
> Offers are made, and students commit to a school (and NCAA) by signing a National Letter of Intent.

Refer to the NCAA website for dates and discuss your plans with your guidance counselor and your coach, as the NCAA timetable varies according to sport and division: www.ncaa.org/wps/wcm/connect/public/NCAA/Resources/Recruiting+Calendars/2012-2013+Recruiting+Calendars.

Arts

Many students who have been involved in visual or performing arts wonder if they should submit an Arts Supplement. If you are applying to arts conservatories, follow those schools' requirements exactly, and submit everything they require. But let's say you are an artist of some kind—a musician, a dancer or performer, or a graphic artist. I'll use photography as an example. If you have submitted your photography to juried arts shows, and especially if you have won prizes at the state, national, or international level, then you want to show colleges the work that won those prizes. But you probably don't need to submit photographs you took in a class in school, unless you continued studying photography after the class was over and have original work that conveys your interest and talent beyond what is required in school.

And if you are planning to study art in college, or audition for theater or music, for each college you should follow the instructions on the Common Application as well as individual colleges' instructions about what to submit, when to submit it, and to whom it should be sent. Arts submissions are usually sent to the relevant departments, and if the professors find someone really promising, they will recommend that person for admission. The departments that usually participate are music, dance, theater, film, and studio arts (creative writing is not applicable). You do not need to submit an Arts Supplement to participate in the program, but a supplement could help you get into the school you want and may help you receive merit-based financial aid. You can submit a tape of a solo performance (or a performance in which you are featured), an art portfolio, or a video on a website like YouTube or Vimeo. A great resource for those attending music, theater, and musical theater auditions is http://auditioningforcollege.wordpress.com/.

Further Reading

Bogart, Anne. *And Then, You Act: Making Art in an Unpredictable World*. New York: Routledge, 2007.

Christensen, Clayton M., and Henry J. Eyring. *The Innovative University*. San Francisco: Jossey-Bass, 2011.

Gendler, J. Ruth. *The Book of Qualities*. New York: Perennial Library, 1988.

Rischard, J. F. *High Noon: Twenty Global Problems, Twenty Years to Solve Them*. New York: Basic Books, 2002.

CHAPTER 12

Write Out Loud

Then I decided I would reclaim my life. I wouldn't let others tell their story of my life. I would tell my own.

—ELYN SAKS[1]

You hear it all the time, and I have harped on it too: college application essays should be "written in your own voice." What does that really mean? "In your own voice" is shorthand for several things:

> Your college application essays should sound like you.
> They should sound like you are talking.
> They should be more like a conversation with a trusted friend than a proclamation to a stranger from a place that is far away.

The exercises in this chapter teach you how to edit to make your essays more like a conversation, and then how to let them go.

REFRESH

Family of Choice

We all have our family of birth, and then as our lives unfold there are people who invite us into their lives, and there are people we invite into ours. For at least 10 minutes, without your pen leaving the paper or your fingers leaving the keyboard, write about your family of choice. This may be specific people you have chosen or who have chosen you, or it may be your ideas about how you will choose or whom you will choose in the future.

The 8-Point Essay Checklist

Here are eight ways to review your essay to heighten the key features of the Moments Method:

1. **Just a moment!** Does the essay explore specific events, or does it remain general?

   Green: There is a specific story that the reader can follow.

   Yellow: There is some effective storytelling, but key aspects of the story happen in the speaker's mind, or it's not always clear how events fit together.

   Red: Your essay is all over the place and lacks focus or specifics.

2. **Is it you?** Is the essay about you? It's fine to write about your grandfather or the teacher who taught you one of life's lessons, but the essay needs to reveal something important about you.

   Green: The essay shows who I am as a person by revealing a unique voice and point of view.

   Yellow: The essay shows me doing interesting things, but it is more about other people than about me.

   Red: The essay is really not about me at all. Nothing about my character is revealed.

3. **You had me at hello.** Does the essay draw the reader in right from the start? Cut out any preambles, introductions, or framing devices left over from the five-paragraph critical essay.

   Green: The first sentence is something the reader will remember weeks later, after reading hundreds of essays.

   Yellow: The first sentence is well written but is still something pretty general that lots of people could have written.

   Red: The first sentence (or sentences) is explanation or filler, not action.

4. **I want more.** Does the essay leave the reader with a feeling that maybe he or she has met you before or wants to meet you in person and learn more about you? Or do you tie everything up in a tidy moral bow that pushes the reader away?

   Green: The last sentence ends in the action and leaves the reader wanting to know more about the writer.

   Yellow: The last sentence ends in the action, but the meaning and importance of the action are not clear.

   Red: The ending is vague, general, or a summary of what you've already shown.

5. **Pack it with action.** Great essays happen in the world, not in the author's mind. Are there action verbs? Is there a strong story line with clear turning points and sense of direction?

Green: The reader is guided through the essay from the author's point of view.

Yellow: The story is interesting, but the direction is unclear.

Red: The story's path is murky and vague.

6. **The three *D*'s—details, dialogue, and description—are there**. Is the story specific? Replace any generalizations with specific sensory descriptions, dialogue, and markers of time and place.

Green: We know where we are in the world and who else is there. Each and every detail adds to the story's direction and purpose.

Yellow: The details are strong, but they do not all add to the point of the story. The descriptions are a bit general. Dialogue is included, but it is not compelling.

Red: Details, dialogue, and description are lacking.

7. **Keep criticism in the classroom.** A great personal essay is very different from the critical essays you learn to write in school. It should reveal who you are and what you believe to anyone, regardless of that person's beliefs. You should not try to change the reader, but connect with him or her.

Green: The reader gets a sense of what you believe and are committed to by experiencing the world from your point of view.

Yellow: Your essay begins to connect, but it still includes a lot of criticism and interpretation.

Red: Your essay tells me what I'm supposed to think—a total turn off.

8. **Who will show up?** Does your essay reveal who you are as a human being? Does it reveal the unique perspective and point of view that you bring to your college community?

Green: I get a clear and compelling picture of who you are and what is important to you through the story you tell about your unique experiences. I want you to come to my college so I can meet you in person!

Yellow: I'm intrigued and would like to know more about you, but there are still a lot of people who sound like you. What can you do to make the story and its message more uniquely your own?

Red: Your writing is vague, general, or filled with scripts that anyone can tell. I don't get any sense of who you are or what is important to you.

You can find an interactive version of this checklist, plus annotated versions of student essays, at www.storytocollege.com/writeoutloud.

In this final round of revisions, pick one or two areas from the checklist where you feel your focused attention will make the biggest improvements in your essay and focus on those as you revise your essay. If you find yourself stuck in the weeds of writing, confused about where to go, try reading the essay out loud—either to a friend or to yourself.

Improvisation, College Apps, and Life

There is no such thing as a mistake.
—HALPERN, CLOSE AND JOHNSON, *TRUTH IN COMEDY*[2]

There are lots of bumps in the road that is the college process. You may wish you worked harder in the class that crushed your GPA. You may try out over and over but still not land a leading role on your school's big stage. You may do everything the best you can and not get into your dream college. Your success in the college process—and in life—flows from your ability to accept whatever life throws at you and like an improv actor on stage say, "Yes, and. . . ."

What do you do when things don't go the way you planned? Do you mope around and let everyone know how miserable you are? Or do you figure out what went wrong, and change what you can so you are more likely to have better results next time? Remember that observer part of your mind I urged you to cultivate in Chapter 1? Studies show that people who are able to observe their own lives—almost as an impartial third-party—and who believe that they can change their outcomes by changing their actions are in fact much more likely to change their outcomes than people who don't believe they have this power.[3] Learning how to change what you are able to in yourself and the world around you is the heart of resilience and ultimately life success. So when you encounter obstacles, use them for learning and things will work out for you in the end.[4]

To step onto the stage of your own life means that you accept whatever happens, and you work with it. *There is no such thing as a mistake.* Whatever happens to you is material to work with and learn from. If you take that approach to college admissions, with a clear vision of landing at a college that's great for you, being yourself as fully as you possibly can, and letting the process unfold, you will be happy. Your best friend may be talking nonstop about college, and your mom may be tearing her hair out with worry (that's a script, by the way), but you will be fine, and you will have a great outcome. You may have a horrible interview but get into the school anyway. You may get sick and miss the national debate championship, and then start some other activity that becomes more important to you. All of this and more will happen, and your first job is to say, "Yes, and. . . ."

Getting into college is the beginning, not the end. Your stage broadens, and your opportunities for learning expand. Not sure what to try first? Any activity that puts you on stage—literally—is a great place to start!

Remember: if you can't read it smoothly out loud, then the reader won't be able to follow it either. Have someone who heard the story told out loud read the finished essay to see if your spoken voice comes through. When you have finished this last round of revision, it's time to show your essay to one or two people for a final review.

Phone a Friend

When you feel an essay is finished—you have gone through the steps, one by one, and you have used stories from your arsenal to answer the particular questions asked by specific colleges—the next step is to have someone else read it. It is important that you maintain control of your essay and keep building on the strengths of your stories and voice, as you have done throughout this book. So when you give a trusted friend or mentor your essay, hand that person these questions to reflect on the work he or she is doing for you:

> Imagine you do not know me. What picture of me does this essay convey to you?
> What are the two or three most important things you learn about me from this essay?
> Is there an area of the essay where you get stuck—you can't follow it, it is confusing, or something is missing? I'm not asking you to jump in and fix it, but I would love to know where you get lost, so I can edit it myself.
> If you find places where this essay drifts into scripts (generalizations that anyone could say), thanks for letting me know where they are, so I can develop them further.
> If you see grammar mistakes or misspellings please show me how to correct them, but thank you for not fixing them for me!

Sometimes you will get to the end of this process and you feel like an essay is just not quite what you want it to be. Set it to the side, go back to your portfolio of stories, and try another story instead. Not every story works for every situation, but if you write college application essays as if you are having a conversation with someone you know and trust, you are starting on sure footing.

Whenever you write, use the unique qualities of your spoken voice, and the issues and experiences that have formed you as a person, and you will connect powerfully with any audience. And when you speak—for interviews, presentations, or any situation where you want people to believe in you—plan out the phrases that you want to use, so you are speaking in a heightened and intentional way, so your writing feels personal rather than formal, and you connect with people in a genuine and intimate way.

Time to Finish

If you have gotten this far, you have done the work to complete powerful college application essays and to perform confidently on the stage of your own life. When you master your stories, you master your life. And when you change your stories, you change your life. So, even if you are sitting in the same blue bedroom writing at the same cracked computer screen where you started, the work you have done in *Write Out Loud* puts you in a different place from where you started—whether that was 12 months ago or 12 days ago.

You are just about done, and the next step is yours! Imagine you have gotten into the college of your dreams. Picture a specific college, and enjoy all the details: the blood red autumn leaves, the hissing of the radiators, the wonderful baggy sweater that your favorite professor wears during office hours. Go to that place and visualize your future. What courses will you study? How will you decorate your dorm room? What new club will you launch? Which lifelong friend will you meet? You deserve spectacular college admissions outcomes; breathe confidently knowing you will achieve them. When you feel ready, take a deep breath, picture the person reading your application with a smile, and then press send. Congratulations!

Gap Year Programs

Deferring college and taking a gap year can be an opportunity to gain perspective, maturity, and experience—and to recharge your batteries after the burnout that is so often the result of students' crazed rush through eleventh and twelfth grades. Many colleges (Harvard included: www.admissions.college.harvard.edu/apply/time_off/index .html) are in favor of students taking a year off before they matriculate. Some even offer organized programs for their students, such as Princeton's Bridge Year program.

If you are considering a gap year, it is strongly advised that you apply to college with your high school class and pay your deposit at your first choice among the colleges to which you are admitted. You should not think of a gap year as a way to beef up your college applications so you will get vastly different outcomes a year later—it almost never works that way, and it would be a horrible waste of a gap year to spend *another* year obsessing about college applications! Your perspective may change during your year off, and you may genuinely want to apply to different types of colleges afterward. Just remember that you must be completely honest with the college where you have made a deposit, and let it know you are applying to other schools and why.

Here are some questions you can ask yourself if you think you may want to consider taking a year off before going to college:

1. **Why do I want to take a gap year?** Are you tired of traditional schooling? Do you feel exhausted and even a bit depressed after high school? Do you want to save some money for your anticipated college expenses? Do you just not feel ready for college? Think about what's motivating you to take a gap year.

2. **What do I want to do and where do I want to go?** Take some time to research the options that are available. What appeals to you? Do you want to be at home or abroad? Do you want to do something academic? Service-oriented? Start writing down the programs and ideas that you like.

3. **What is my plan?** There are many established gap year programs (see Further Reading on Gap Years following for a few of them), but you can also design your own gap year by mixing and matching programs or creating your own plan from scratch. Your plan should be comprehensive, and you should account for all travel and accommodations.

4. **How much will it cost?** Depending on where you go and what you do, a gap year can cost almost as much as a year in college. If you find a job or a paid internship, however, taking a year off might be a money-saver. Create a budget for your gap year and determine what is feasible.

5. **How will my gap year prepare me for college and life after college?** This is really the most important question of all: not what am I leaving, but what am I pursuing and how will that contribute to my overall learning and professional opportunities?

EXAMPLES OF ORGANIZED GAP YEAR PROGRAMS
> AmeriCorps: www.americorps.gov/
> Carpe Diem Education: www.carpediemeducation.org/home.php
> Global Citizen Year: http://globalcitizenyear.org
> Global Gap Program: www.projects-abroad.org/volunteer-projects/gap-year/overview
> Leap Now: http://leapnow.org/
> National Outdoor Leadership School: www.nols.edu/
> Where There Be Dragons: www.wheretherebedragons.com/

For more options, search Teen Life: www.teenlife.com/pages/gap-year-programs/. Yale also has a list of resources: www.yale.edu/yalecollege/international/welcome/gap_year.html.

Further Reading on Gap Years

Haigler, Karl, and Rae Nelson. *The Gap Year Advantage: Helping Your Child Benefit from Time Off Before or During College.* New York: St. Martin's Griffin, 2005.

Wood, Danielle. *The Uncollege Alternative: Your Guide to Incredible Careers and Amazing Adventures Outside College.* New York: Regan Books, 2000.

Further Reading

Ganz, Marshall. "What Is Public Narrative?" Working Paper, Kennedy School of Government, Harvard University, 2008.

Halpern, Charna, Del Close, and Kim Johnson. *Truth in Comedy: The Manual of Improvisation.* Colorado Springs, Colorado: Meriwether Publishing, 1994.

Lamott, Anne. *Bird by Bird: Some Instructions on Writing and Life.* New York: Anchor Books, 1995.

PART 4

MORE TOOLS FOR YOUR JOURNEY

CHAPTER 13

Sound Smarter
How to Find and Fix 10 Common Grammar Glitches

You should take the time to ensure that your spelling is correct and your grammar is error-free. Here are some common grammatical mistakes that you definitely want to avoid.

1. **Is it a full sentence? Is it one sentence or two sentences spliced together with a comma?**
   Problem: *I hate breakfast, I like lunch.*
   Solutions: *I hate lunch, but I like dinner. I hate breakfast; I like lunch.*

2. **The subject and verb of a sentence need to agree; both need to be either singular or plural.**
   Problem: *The birds was pretty*
   Solution: *The birds were pretty.*

3. **Is it plural or possessive?**
   a. Plural: The plural of *word* is *words*, not *word's*. *The words in the manuscript were in medieval French.*
   b. Possessive: *That word's meaning is a mystery to me.*

4. **Do you mean *its* or *it's*?**
   a. *Its* means "belonging to it": *The bird expanded its wings and took off.*
   b. *It's* is a contraction of "it is": *It's time to go home.* (Note: Unless you are quoting someone's exact words, you should expand "it's" to "it is.")

5. **Check for *there* vs. *their* vs. *they're*.**
   a. *There* can be either an adverb (referring to a place) or a pronoun in phrases like "there is": *Look, over there, it's a fire station.*
   b. *Their* is a possessive pronoun referring to a group: *The firefighters are practicing their drills.*
   c. *They're* is a contraction for "they are" or "they were": *They're all dressed in their uniforms.* (Note: *They're* is a contraction and, unless you are quoting someone, should not be used in written work.)

6. **Replace *could of/should of/would of* with *could have/should have/would have*.**

7. **Many people confuse *affect* and *effect*.**
   a. *Affect* is a verb: *The temperature affected my performance in the race.*
   b. *Effect* is a noun: *I could feel the effects of the heat as I ran. The effects of the BP oil spill will affect wildlife in the gulf for decades.*

8. **Should it be *two* or *to* or *too*?**
   a. *To* is a preposition: *I drove to the racetrack.*
   b. *Too* is an adverb: *There were too many people there.*
   c. *Two* is a number: *I could not see the two winning horses.*

9. ***I* before *e*, except after *c*, or when it sounds like *a* as in *neighbor* or *weigh*.**

10. **Check for homonyms—words that sound alike but mean different things.** Examples:

    Flower (garden) vs. *flour* (kitchen)
    Way (path) vs. *weigh* (what a scale does)
    Flecks (spots) vs. *flex* (muscles)

    This is something autocorrect will not fix, and may even make worse. Confused? Check a dictionary to make sure you are using the words you mean.

CHAPTER 14

Preparing for Interviews

Y ou should always meet your interviewer in a public place. To prepare for your interview, Refresh—write down all the things that are cluttering your brain—from AP homework you haven't finished to those new jeans you want but can't afford—and let it all go.

1. **Who are you?** Make a list of two or three things you want the interviewer to learn about you. What makes you different from people who—on paper—look pretty much the same?

2. **Use stories to connect.** This is the fun part! Let's say you want to demonstrate courage. Think of stories that show your courage, without having to say, "I'm courageous." Sometimes we overlook the obvious; what do you do every day that is courageous in your own way?

3. **Share the details.** Which one of these stories are you most likely to remember? Which one would you put on your résumé? Which is most likely to connect with someone if you are talking to him or her face-to-face?

   > "I organized a really big fund-raising event."
   > "I started my school's first Dance Marathon for cancer research. We raised $25,413 and involved 126 students and faculty."
   > "It was 6:56 in the morning, 4 minutes 'til the end. I leaned over to my sweaty partner and said, 'I can't believe a year ago this was just an idea. There are more than 100 people here. Hannah would be so happy!' "

4. **Own the space.** When you walk into an interview, do you become a bit dizzy or short of breath? That happens to everyone; it's just the reptile part of your brain's "fight or flight" response kicking in. Just keep breathing and walking. Look around and say to yourself, "I own this space," and with a gentle smile and wide-open eyes, reach out to shake the interviewer's hand.

5. **Where are you?** Research each school you are visiting. Imagine yourself as part of the community, and speak honestly from that place. For instance, "Last summer I worked in a neuroscience lab at NYU. Your website describes opportunities for undergraduate research. Can you tell me some more about that?"

6. **Expect the expected.** Prepare answers for the most likely questions: Why do you want to apply to this college? What do you want to major in? Tell me about your strengths and weaknesses.

7. **Who is your interviewer?** Connect with the interviewer as a person. Did the person go to the college? How long has he or she worked in admissions? Ask something that you really want to know!

8. **Ask something new.** Come up with a question that's really your own. Consider it a success when your interviewer says, "Wow, never heard that one before!"

9. **Be ready for "the stumper."** Some interviewers pride themselves on throwing out an occasional "curveball question." If you find yourself facing a question you've never considered before, give yourself some time. Be honest and say, "You know, I've never thought about that before!" or "Wow, I don't think anyone's ever asked me that before." Then take a few seconds to think. It will feel like forever to you, but to your interviewer, it will just be a pause in which you appeared thoughtful.

10. **Follow up.** Write a thank-you note, and mail it right away (even if you send an e-mail, a handwritten note will be opened, read, and remembered). If the interviewer asked for something (your journalism portfolio or more information about summer courses), make sure to send it.

11. **Remember that nothing is carved in stone.** In those rare instances in which you *do* say something that, upon further reflection, you think might not have come out the way you wanted, your thank-you note can be a perfect opportunity to circle back and add a little more context. "As soon as I got into my dad's car, I realized that what you were probably asking was. . . ."

12. **And whatever happens, let it go because that one is over and done!** Learn for the next one, and give yourself a pat on the back.

CHAPTER 15

Frequently Asked Questions

hen I speak at schools, following are the questions students most often ask me.

1. **When should I start working on my application essays?**
   The best time to complete your application essays is the summer before senior year. But the sooner you learn the tools to complete personal essays the better, since you need them to apply for summer programs and scholarships as well as college applications. Many students take Story To College courses the summer after tenth grade and begin exploring possible stories then. The spring of junior year is packed with responsibilities—SATs or ACTs, Honors projects, and AP tests—but in February and March before you get too crazed, take a look at The Bridge (Chapter 2) and start thinking about what you want colleges to know about you: both what you've already done and what you want to do in college. The winter and spring are relatively quiet times in your college advisor's office, so it's a great time to start a conversation there and enlist your advisor in your research and planning. Bring The Bridge chart to that meeting, and start to share your hopes and dreams with your advisor, so he or she can help you achieve them.

2. **Are there topics I just shouldn't write about?**
   The standard answer to this question is don't write about death, disease, and divorce. But I have found that the very topics that cry out "Essay Danger Zone" can also be successfully answered. Sometimes you need to think and write through these personally painful subjects to figure out if you want to write about them in your college applications.

3. **What about the 650-word limit? How serious is that?**
   In the new 2013–2014 Common Application ("CA4") there is a mandatory essay length of 250 to 650 words. The online application will not accept essays shorter than 250 or longer than 650 words.

4. **What if I'm not sure what I want to study in college? How should I answer the question about my intended major?**

   You can always say you are "Undecided," but I recommend you explore some different options. Talk to people of different ages and stages of life about their careers, and how they connected the dots between college and career. You will learn many things about yourself and the work world in the process! And then you can answer the question with specific details about different majors you are considering.

5. **Can Dungeons and Dragons be considered an extracurricular activity? Seriously?**

   Yes! In college application essays you should present yourself and express yourself as the person you are!

6. **Is it appropriate to write about an ethically debated topic—such as hacking—if it's your hobby?**

   This could be a great topic, especially if you use "hacking" for social good. The trick would be to take your reader to a moment you understand to be ethically questionable and show how you negotiated it. I would love to read this essay!

7. **How much parent involvement in the process is too much?**

   Parents who find themselves starting sentences about their student's college process with the pronoun *we* are probably heading into unhealthy territory. I once heard an admissions officer say that in this process the student needs to be the driver. Parents are going to be tempted to take the wheel, but it's important for them to be focused on the ultimate goal of the student's successfully independent life. Students and parents need to talk about identifying the line between helping and taking over, and working hard to respect that boundary. Parents are absolutely part of the process, and in many ways the final decision about where the student will matriculate is a family decision . . . but it is the student who will be attending college, after all. Parents can try out for the role of trusted GPS, but they need to leave the driving to the student.

8. **I've heard that the essay is the last thing the admissions reviewer reads. Is that true?**

   Most admissions counselors I know say that they read the essay either first or last to provide perspective and detail to the rest of the folder.

9. **How fast do admissions reviewers read your essay? How many per day?**

   In the first round, they may spend a couple of minutes on your essay, or they may not read it at all, depending on what else is in your folder. But in situations where they are deciding between candidates who are similar, the process slows down and the essay often provides vital information to distinguish you from candidates who otherwise look similar on paper.

10. **What exactly are admissions officers looking for?**

    Each college has its own algorithm for evaluating applications. You can find detailed information on each college's website and by talking with admissions counselors when they visit your school or you visit theirs. Most colleges look for students who are a good fit for their programs and community, so make sure you really research the schools you are applying to before you spend a lot of time working on their applications and supplements.

11. **Can I write about something that happened to me a long time ago?**

    Yes, you can definitely write about experiences that were important to you and happened when you were young. If you can bring the essay into the present somehow, and put the experience from the past in current perspective, that will help the reader understand how this experience affects who you will be in college.

12. **I had a really rough time with friends and self-esteem junior year, and my grades suffered. Should I write about this in my personal essay?**

    Probably not. Use the 650-word personal essay to showcase your learning and growth. You might ask your guidance counselor to write about this situation, or you can include a brief, matter-of-fact explanation in the Additional Information section.

13. **What if my stories don't relate to my major and career goals?**

    The role of the Personal Essay is to reveal who you are as a person. For the short answers about major and career plans, you will want to look for connections between what you have done in the past and the possible careers you see for yourself in the future. No one expects you to have your whole life figured out at age 18!

14. **What are the most predictable and overworked topics?**

    These include overcoming minor challenges, giving leftover food to homeless people in a third-world country, and expensive service trips.

15. **What should I do when I have writer's block?**

    Do a quick Refresh, and then free-write for at least 10 minutes, where you just write everything you can think of without letting your pen leave the paper or your fingers leave the keyboard.

16. **Can I use the same topic for more than one essay for the same school?**

    No. Try to use each essay to reveal a different aspect of your character and story. It's especially dangerous to use the same experience—say a school service trip to Costa Rica—to answer more than one question.

17. **I want to write about being LGBT, but my mom says I shouldn't. What can I do?**

    Your mom may be afraid you will be discriminated against in the admissions process, but that is unlikely. I would say that this is really your decision, but it would be great if you could have a conversation with your mom and figure out where she's coming from.

18. **I've heard that a great essay can make up for other gaps in your academic record. Is that true?**

No, that is generally not true. If you are really not academically qualified for a school, the best essay on the planet is unlikely to tip an admissions decision in your favor.

19. **Can I submit an essay I wrote for English class with my applications instead of a Personal Essay?**

No, Personal Essays follow a completely different format from the critical essays you write for English class. Unless the college specifically gives you this option, it's better not to use school papers in place of Personal Essays.

20. **What is the kiss of death in college essays?**

Anything that seems like the student did not take the time to do his or her best work is the kiss of death, including typos, major grammar or spelling mistakes, and obvious bloopers. Vague, general or self-promotional essays are also not good. A fire hose of either unfiltered emotions or harsh and judgmental opinions also usually sends the reader packing. Worst of all is an essay that sounds like it was written by a 40-something consultant rather than a flesh and blood young person.

The Common Application is an online college application shared by more than 500 colleges and universities in the United States and abroad. Developed over 35 years, the Common App is free and can be accessed online (www.commonapp.org). It serves as the foundation of the college application process for most selective colleges and universities.

The Common Application has recently been revised, and the new version was released online on August 1, 2013. The new design is intuitive and user-friendly, and there is a lot of built-in support for applicants. You can download a sample copy of the new 2013–2014 Common App at www.commonapp.org/CommonApp/DownloadForms.aspx.

Most US colleges and universities—even ones that do not use the Common App—use a format that is similar to the Common App, so this guide will help you to navigate other online applications as well.

What exactly do you need to be prepared for when you fill out the Common App? It includes these sections:

PROFILE
> Contacts
> Demographics
> Geography

FAMILY
> Parent and/or guardian
> Siblings

EDUCATION
> Current school
> School history
> Academic information (GPA, class rank, schedule, honors, and awards)

TESTING
> College entrance (SAT and/or ACT)
> English for non-native speakers
> Academic subject tests (SAT II, AP, IB, etc.)
> Other (optional)

ACTIVITIES/WORK
> Years of participation
> Hours per week and weeks per year
> Position/leadership held (50 characters)
> Brief description (150 characters)

ESSAY
> You will select one of five essay choices to write about. See the essay choices on page 247.

EXPLANATIONS
> Required responses (school discipline, criminal history, educational interruption)

ADDITIONAL INFORMATION
> Optional responses (circumstances not reflected elsewhere)

COLLEGE PAGE 1 (formally a separate supplement for each college, the questions will vary from school to school)
> General
  * Entry term
  * Degree status
  * Housing preference
  * Test-optional (if applicable)
  * Scholarship (if applicable)
  * Financial aid preference
> Academic program
> Previous contact with institution (interview, visit)
> Family members who attended institution
> Evaluations (names of recommenders)
> Residence
> Signature (acknowledgments and affirmations)

COLLEGE PAGE 2
> Writing supplement: College-specific essays and short answers

SECTIONS FOR YOUR SCHOOL TO COMPLETE
> Counselor recommendation
> Teacher recommendations
> Mid-year report (sent to colleges in January)
> Transcript(s)

Tips for Completing the Common Application

Here are my tips for completing the new Common App and also the supplements if you are applying to colleges that require them.

1. **Get started early.** The Common Application is released on August 1 each year. You can get a jumpstart by printing out the application in advance and gathering all of the family and financial information. Get organized by making a list or spreadsheet, see the next page, of all the information you need to give to or gather from others to complete the Common Application. You can also download this form at www.story tocollege.com/writeoutloud.

2. **Request teachers' recommendations.** Depending on which colleges you are applying to, you will need one or two teachers' recommendations. It's best to request recommendations from teachers who know your work well, ideally teachers whose courses you took in eleventh or twelfth grade.

   > Schedule a conversation. In the spring of junior year or early fall of senior year talk to your teachers and ask if any would be willing to write you a positive letter of recommendation. If any teacher says no, respect that, learn from it, and find someone else.
   > Come prepared. It's fine to give your teacher a short list of talking points—for instance, the time he or she gave you three extra books to read that changed how you approached your final paper for the course. But never write the letter for your teacher, or ask him or her to write it a certain way.
   > Have a backup plan. If a teacher tells you that he or she cannot write you a positive recommendation or does not know you very well, thank the teacher for being honest and ask a different teacher for a recommendation.
   > Should I send another letter? If there is someone outside your school who knows your work particularly well—for example, a college professor whose course you took or who advised your advanced research, or someone you worked with closely in a job or internship—you might consider submitting a third letter of recommendation. But this is entirely optional and not required, and it is better *not* to submit a letter if the person does not know you well.

3. **Request counselor's recommendation and school transcript(s).** You need to request an official transcript from each high school or college you have attended. It can take a week or more for schools to process your transcript requests, so allow plenty of time. A week before your applications are due, it's a good idea check with each school to make sure they have sent out your transcripts. If there are any anomalies in your record, you should speak frankly to your counselor about how these will be addressed. You should also speak to these issues directly—not in your main essay, but on a separate page called Additional Information (see What to Include in the Additional Information Section, on page 251).

College Application Organizer

College or University	Decision Type	Due Date	SAT/ ACT	SAT subject tests	Do they accept the Common App?	Are you applying to a specific program?
Example: UNC	Early Action	10/7/2016	Optional	1	Yes	Honors Program

Financial Aid Forms	Arts or Athletic Supplement	Supplement	Supplement Essay 1	Supplement Essay 2	Supplement Essay 3	Recommendations needed	Other	Completed	Submitted
Yes	None	Yes	Issue			1	Interview Recommended	No	No

Common App FAQs by Section

Before you get started, here are some frequently asked questions about completing various sections of the Common Application, which may help you.

What if I don't know what my future academic interests are?

On the online version of the Common Application, there is a dropdown menu. One of the options is "Undecided"; this is the one you may want to select on this section.

Will my academic interests affect my admission to the university or college?

Yes and no. Colleges and universities want students who will study in their key departments, so they may take special interest in your application based on what you choose. However, what you put here will not determine your admissions outcome; it is just one of many factors colleges consider. So be honest about what you think you want to study in college, knowing that more than 60 percent of students change their majors at least once in their first two years of college! And don't forget that several colleges offer independent majors that allow students to fashion their own programs.

But if I choose "Undecided" for my academic interests, does that make me look bad or unprepared?

Not at all! Most students change their minds about their majors once they take actual college classes in different departments; admissions counselors know this. At the same time, if your high school academic background, extracurricular activities, and writing clearly show an inclination toward a certain subject, feel free to write that down and describe how that course of study has been important to you.

What if I want to change from one program to another—say from Engineering to Liberal Arts—once I'm in college?

Check on each college's website to determine the process and requirements for transferring from one program to another after you have been admitted.

Applicant Information

What if I don't have a US Social Security Number?

The Common App will prompt you to upload a copy of your green card or proof of refugee status. If you want to be considered for federal financial aid via FAFSA, you must include your social security number.

What if I have two permanent addresses, one with each parent?

Write down the address of the home at which you spend the most time. Later, under "Family," you will have a chance to write down your other address as well.

What if I do not use my home phone number?

Write down your preferred telephone number (i.e., check the circle that says "cell"), and then provide that number.

Demographics

Do I have to write down my religion and ethnic background?

No. This part of the Demographics section is optional. However, you do need to write down your citizenship status, birthplace, and years lived in the United States.

Why do colleges ask for this information?

Colleges are interested in the diversity of applicants and enrolled students. This information will not be used in a discriminatory manner in the admissions process.

What if I am more than one of the ethnic options provided on the Common App?

You are allowed to check more than one.

Family

What if I don't know the date of my parents' divorce?

Try to find this information from one of your parents. Only the month and year are required.

My parents are divorced and one of my parents does not provide child support, so he/she is basically out of contact. Do I still have to write down his/her information?

The Parent section is especially important when colleges are considering financial aid. You should try to provide your parent's information, but talk to your guidance counselor, so your counselor can include details about your family situation in his or her recommendation. Your guidance counselor is an advocate for you in the admissions process, so make sure you discuss the issue with your counselor. Otherwise, colleges have no way of knowing about your specific circumstances.

What if my parent(s) did not attend college?

Either leave the question blank, or choose the option that is closest to "not applicable."

If I have step- or half-brothers and -sisters, do I include their information in the "Siblings" section as well?

Yes. This section may be especially important if another sibling is attending college or university at the same time, as this may affect your eligibility for financial aid. You may indicate that he or she is a step- or half-brother or -sister where it says "Relationship."

Education

I'm in high school, why would they ask me for colleges and universities I've attended?

Some students have had the opportunity to attend enrichment programs at universities or have decided to take college level courses during high school. This section is for students who have attended either of these types of courses on a college campus.

Why do colleges ask for this information?

Colleges are interested in your experience of college-level coursework as it reflects on your ability to succeed in college. Remember to request a copy of your transcript for these courses, if they are not already on your high school transcript.

Academics

Note that if you drop or change any of the senior year courses you list in this section, your guidance counselor needs to tell colleges that you have changed your course of study and must explain the reasons why.

My school does not have a class rank. What do I do?

Admissions counselors understand that some schools do not calculate class rank. Indicate the class size, but choose N/A for class rank. Colleges receive a school profile of your high school from your guidance counselor, so they will know that your school does not rank students.

I sent my SAT scores via the College Board. Do I have to indicate my scores here too?

Yes.

It asks for AP/IB scores. Do I need to submit these separately or just list them here?

You do *not* need to submit separate AP/IB scores. Just list them in the Academics section.

I have taken different levels of classes during high school. Should I indicate this on the Common App?

Yes. If you are taking AP or IB courses, indicate those first under "Current Courses," followed by accelerated/honors courses, other courses, and so on. Admission counselors will receive a copy of your transcript, but they also thoroughly read the Common Application and will want to see the level of academic rigor in your course schedule.

I do not have any honors from high school. Do I leave this section blank?

Yes. But remember this section includes honors at the school, state/regional, national, and international levels. If you have received something like a School Spirit Award or a Citizenship Award from your school, these are honors you may include!

Disciplinary History

I have been put on probation/suspension/removal/dismissal/expulsion from my high school before. I clicked "yes," and then the Common App prompted me to a blank page to write about the experience. Do I have to do that?

Yes. Some colleges will not consider an application if the student does not explain what the situation was or what he or she learned from the experience. If you say nothing it may make it seem you are not taking responsibility for your disciplinary violations. Make sure you complete this section, as admissions counselors know that the Common App prompts you directly to a page to write about your disciplinary history if you mark "yes". Talk to your guidance counselor about how to craft this statement.

Activities (Includes Extracurricular Activities and Work Experience)

Does the order of my activities or work experience matter?

The directions say to write your activities in the order of importance to you. Admissions counselors will assume that the activity you write first is the one that matters most to you.

What am I supposed to write on the top and bottom lines?

On the top, indicate the position/name of employer or company/honors (e.g., varsity basketball co-captain; busboy at La Strada Pizzeria; Bronze medalist for Latin Competition; part-time secretary at Horizons Inc.). On the bottom, write the description of what you did (e.g., led team to win the State Championships in 2012; set tables, managed cleanliness of back room and maintained restaurant inventory; participated in the National Latin Competition for Intermediate level students; filed papers, managed company calendar, and organized events).

What if I don't remember how many hours or weeks I spent doing each activity?

Try your best to make an accurate estimate. You want to show colleges how committed you were to the activities in which you participated during high school.

I have no work experience because I am always home taking care of my siblings. Do I just leave this section blank?

No! That is an extracurricular activity! Taking care of your siblings could be considered a part-time job, especially if you spend a lot of hours doing it. Admissions counselors understand that students have a variety of responsibilities outside of school that may prevent them from fully engaging in other types of extracurricular activities. Write down how many hours per week you spend taking care of your siblings, and make sure you indicate during which grades you did this as well as when during the year it happened (i.e., school year and/or summer break).

Signature and Payment

You also need to sign your Common Application electronically and state that all of the work you are submitting is your own and true. After you have completed the Writing section, as well as the Supplement for each college, you can pay by credit card to submit the application online to that college. If applying to college presents a financial hardship to you or your family, you can apply through your guidance counselor for a waiver on the cost of applying to college. You have to apply for this waiver only once, and it will be used for all your applications.

Writing (aka The Personal Essay)

The 2013–2014 Common Application (CA4) has five essay choices:

> Some students have a background or story that is so central to their identity that they believe their application would be incomplete without it. If this sounds like you, then please share your story.

> Recount an incident or time when you experienced failure. How did it affect you, and what lessons did you learn?

> Reflect on a time when you challenged a belief or idea. What prompted you to act? Would you make the same decision again?

> Describe a place or environment where you are perfectly content. What do you do or experience there, and why is it meaningful to you?

> Discuss an accomplishment or event, formal or informal, that marked your transition from childhood to adulthood within your culture, community, or family.

The instructions say, "The essay demonstrates your ability to write clearly and concisely on a selected topic and helps you distinguish yourself in your own voice. What do you want the readers of your application to know about you apart from courses, grades, and test scores? Choose the option that best helps you answer that question and write an essay of no more than 650 words, using the prompt to inspire and structure your response. Remember: 650 words is your limit, not your goal. Use the full range if you need it, but don't feel obligated to do so. (The application won't accept a response shorter than 250 words.)"

10 STEPS TO AWESOME APPLICATION ESSAYS

1. **Refresh: Clear your mind of doubts and distractions**. Studies show that your best writing happens when you create a space to write that is free from tension, worry, and other distractions. Before you start writing take a few minutes to create a space that is free from other work and any doubts you may have about the admissions process. There are many ways to refresh: you can exercise or take a short walk outside; or write about what's on your mind and throw it away; or just take a few breaths and let yourself relax before you start to work on your essays.

2. **Build a Bridge: Find great topics from your own experience.** In college application essays you show colleges what you will do in the future based on what you have already done. So take a piece of paper and draw a line down the middle; on the left side of the page write "My Life Story," and on the right write "Where I Am Going." Start with the "Where I Am Going" side and write at least 10 things that you want to do in college, work, and the rest of your life. Then, on the "My Life Story" side, list at least 10 things that you want colleges to know about you, especially the experiences that have shaped you into who you are today and who you want to be in the future. Explore the connection between what you have already done and where you want to go in the future. Are there any experiences that naturally connect your past to your future?

3. **Transform Scripts to Stories: Tell the stories only you can tell.** Take another look at the 20 things you wrote in step 2. Are any of them very general things that lots of people can say—clichés like "I'm ambitious" or "I want to be an engineer?" At Story To College we call that general type of writing "scripts." There's nothing wrong with scripts; that's how most people talk most of the time. But scripts don't help to distinguish you from anyone else. Wherever you have scripts, you want to replace them with specific stories that only you can tell. You accomplish this by expanding individual moments from your experience to find actions, dialogue, and details. Let's say your moment involves a lesson you learned when your father became upset with you. Lots of people's fathers get upset, but they do it in different ways. Did he stand in the window looking down at you and, without words, motion for you to come inside (action)? Did he quietly say, "Get home" (dialogue)? Did he walk behind you the whole way home as you stared down at the dusty sidewalks (detail)? There are examples of personal stories from great writers on the Story To College website (www.storytocollege.com/writeoutloud). For each script you identify from step 2, try to find at least two or three specific stories.

4. **Choose a Moment: Avoid the two most common mistakes.** Mistake #1 is trying to pack too much into your application essay. Remember, the goal of a college application essay is to show who you are as a human being, beyond your grades and test scores. Your scores, accomplishments, and awards all have other places on the application; so use the essays to reveal something new about you. Pick one of the stories from step 3, and explore it in more detail. Let's say your story is about the child your family adopted when you were 12. There are many parts to that story: your parents told you they were going to adopt a child; you went to meet the child in Russia; she was just a year older than you and shared your bedroom. Include as many details as you can remember; take as much space as you need. Then pick *one* of those moments where you risked something, learned something, changed, or grew in some way.

Mistake #2 is focusing on thoughts rather than actions. You will be tempted to start off your story with something like "I realized . . ." or "I thought . . ." or "I felt. . . ." You connect with the reader more powerfully by allowing the reader to draw conclusions about you. Neuroscience research shows that when people listen to a story there are three immediate responses: their brains trigger memories of similar stories; they feel empathy; and they have a desire to take action. By telling the reader what to think, it prevents these responses. In the next step you will tell your story out loud. Stick to the actions, dialogue, and details to show your reader what you realized, thought, or felt.

5. **Tell It Out Loud: Speak so admissions will listen.** One of the main things admissions officers are looking for is an authentic voice. Tell your story out loud to a small group of friends and record your own storytelling. By recording your story you can capture the unique qualities of your spoken voice as well as the specific details that you remember when talking. After you are finished telling the story, let your friends ask you questions and record those too.

6. **Write It Out: Find the gold in your spoken word.** Listen to your recording from step 5 and transcribe your story word for word. The goal is to use your spoken voice to strengthen your writing and also to learn more about how you sound when you speak. So be sure to include all of the "ums" and "likes." Then, print out a hard copy of your story and highlight in green the places where your story is strongest. Highlight in orange places where your spoken voice is strongest (they may overlap). And highlight in yellow places where the story includes language that is vague, general, or could be said by lots of other people.

7. **Heighten the Three _D_'s: Use details, description, and dialogue.** Anywhere you highlighted in yellow in step 6, replace general statements with specific sensory details (things you experience through sight, sound, smell, taste, and touch), physical description (orient the reader in time and space), and dialogue (the actual words people say). For instance replace "It was a really nice day" with "It was the first day of spring, and the orange tulips had just started blooming in our front yard. My mom said, 'It's perfect weather for your lacrosse game.'"

8. **Map It: Structure your essay with a strong story arc.** Does your essay have a clear beginning, middle, and end? We call them Magnet, Pivot, and Glow. What do you want your reader to learn about you from this story? What action will leave your reader with that idea? That is the Glow, and the end of the story. What action in the middle of the story resulted in that end? That's your Pivot. And where did the action start? That's the Magnet that draws your reader in. Be very specific; create a three-sentence map of the key elements of your story and then go back into each section and choose the details, dialogue, and description that move the story forward.

9. **Magnet and Glow: Create memorable beginnings and endings.** The beginning of your essay should draw the reader in like a magnet, and the last sentence should leave them with the glow of wanting to know more about you. You can heighten

your Magnet by putting your reader in the action, prompting your reader to ask, "What's next," or setting the scene. And you can strengthen your Glow by keeping your reader in the action, leaving more to be asked, or closing the scene.

10. **Write Out Loud: Revise to emphasize your unique voice.** Here's an eight-point checklist to guide your essay revision:
    > Does the essay take the reader to a specific place and moment in time?
    > Does the essay reveal something important about you?
    > Does the first sentence draw the reader in?
    > Does the last sentence leave the reader wanting to know more about you?
    > Does the essay include actions that happen in the world?
    > Are general phrases replaced with specific details, dialogue, and description?
    > Is the voice welcoming to everyone, whether or not they agree with you?
    > Does the essay show something important about who you will be in a college community?

Writing FAQs

The essay directions say I can write between 250 and 650 words. That means I can write just 250 words, right?
Sure, you can. But the Personal Essay is your chance to speak to the admissions counselors in your own voice. The rest of your application says what you did, how long you did it, and what you achieved. After grades and SATs, the essays are the most important part of your application. Use these essays to paint a fuller picture of yourself and show colleges your personality! Take advantage of the essays to reveal your unique character and point of view.

How personal should the Personal Essay be?
Here's our rule of thumb: if you were in the room talking to this person you are meeting for the first time, is this a story you would tell? Is this how you would tell it if your goal is to continue the conversation with that person? In our always-connected world, a lot of very raw writing circulates in cyberspace without much pause for reflection. It's important to be honest and genuine in your essays, and it is fine to share moments that reveal what matters to you, even to show times when you have made mistakes. Whenever possible shape your essays to show the reader how you have grown and changed as well as what you have learned and done as a result of these experiences.

Shouldn't I write about awards or accomplishments?
Your academic awards and extracurricular accomplishments will show up in other parts of your application. Use the essays to add more information, to reveal who you are as a person.

How do you fit everything important in 650 words?

You can't! In 250 to 650 words you can only write about one thing. It is much more powerful to tell one important story than to try to tell your whole life story in 650 words.

How important is it that my essay be polished?

Admissions officers look for authenticity, not slickly polished essays. It's much better to write in a voice that is your own than to smooth over your essay into something that anyone can write. While you don't want to edit out your unique voice, you do want to proofread for spelling and grammar and take time to make sure the essays represent your best work.

Hasn't anything I might write about already been written by thousands of other students?

Many students participate in community service. Many students travel. And many students play sports. But you are the only person who has had your experiences. Often the best essays come from common everyday experiences that reveal your character and humanity. Take those general experiences and focus on moments that are really your own.

What do college admissions officers say I should write about?

There are no pre-set "good topics." Start with your own experiences, and use those experiences to show who you will be in college and in life.

What to Include in the Additional Information Section

In the new 2013–2014 Common Application (CA4), the Additional Information section will prompt you to write about any relevant circumstances or qualifications that are not reflected in the rest of the application. The new section will not accept attachments. Following are some possible items to include in this section:

> You can discuss a significant outside activity (such as service or leadership at the state or national level) that is not fully described elsewhere.

> This is also the place to address—directly and matter-of-factly—any circumstances that may have affected your academic performance.

> You can use the Additional Information section to speak frankly about any unusual circumstances in your school record or personal life. No drama, no apologies; a matter-of-fact tone is best. For example,

> Spring of my sophomore year was a really rough time for me and my family. My father lost his job, and my little sister was diagnosed with leukemia. As you can see on my transcript, my grades suffered that term. Over time, I've learned how to manage schoolwork, activities, and family responsibilities much better, and I feel really well prepared to balance all the different parts of college life.

Supplements Specific to Each College

Many colleges have additional essay questions included in College Page 2 of the Common Application. And many include important additional information about their supplements on their websites.

These supplements are really important! This is the place where you can connect with each college by researching their programs and talking specifically about how you will engage as a student and community member. Successful supplements take time and research. Plan ahead so you have time to write specific essays for each college to which you are applying.

> **Use each essay to reveal a different aspect of your character and experience.** Don't reuse your Personal Essay for your supplement essays (e.g., don't write multiple essays about the same trip to Brazil).

> **Make each supplement a conversation with that specific college.** Research the colleges to which you are applying and connect with each one honestly. Reveal the depth of your character, your intellectual curiosity, the impact you had on your local community, and the impact the community has had on you. Imagine you are a student at that college, and talk about how you will take advantage of its programs and make a difference in its community.

FREE RESOURCES FOR STUDENTS AND PARENTS

COLLEGE SEARCH

Big Future: http://bigfuture.collegeboard.org

College Express: www.collegexpress.com/college/search

Fiske, Edward. *The Fiske Guide to Colleges 2014*. Naperville, IL: Sourcebooks, 2013.

Noodle: www.noodle.org

Zinch: www.zinch.com

TEST PREP

ACT or SAT?: www.kaptest.com/pdf_files/college/sat-act-practice-test.pdf

SAT Practice Test: http://sat.collegeboard.org/practice/sat-practice-test

ACT Practice Test: www.actstudent.org/sampletest

The Official SAT Study Guide. 2nd ed. New York: College Board, 2009.

The Real ACT Prep Guide: the Only Official Prep Guide from the Makers of the ACT. Lawrenceville, NJ: Peterson's, 2008.

FINANCIAL AID

Cappex: www.cappex.com

Chany, Kalman A., and Geoff Martz. *Paying for College Without Going Broke*. 2013 ed. New York: Random House, 2012.

College Greenlight: www.collegegreenlight.com

CSS Profile: http://student.collegeboard.org/css-financial-aid-profile

FAFSA: www.fafsa.ed.gov

FastWeb: www.fastweb.com

USA Government Financial Aid: http://studentaid.ed.gov

Zinch: www.zinch.com

NOTES

ACKNOWLEDGMENTS

1. Carol Barash, *English Women's Poetry 1649–1714: Politics, Community, and Linguistic Authority* (Oxford, UK: Oxford University Press, 1996).

INTRODUCTION TO THE 12 TOOLS

1. Lawrence G. Smith, *Cesare Pavese and America: Life, Love, and Literature* (Amherst: University of Massachusetts Press, 2008), 92.

2. In his book *The Storytelling Animal,* Jonathan Gottschall poses the question: If storytelling is a luxury, then why hasn't natural selection eliminated it? He concludes that storytelling is a biologically necessary part of being human. Jonathan Gottschall, *The Storytelling Animal: How Stories Make Us Human* (New York: Houghton Mifflin Harcourt, 2012), 21–44.

3. Learning over a long period of time is known as "distributed learning" as opposed to "massed learning," which describes processing a lot of information in a short amount of time. Leib Litman and Lila Davachi's 2008 study concluded that distributive learning is more effective than massed learning. According to the study, distributive learning slows the rate of forgetting. See Leib Litman and Lila Davachi, "Distributed Learning Enhances Relational Memory Consolidated," *Learning and Memory* 15 (2008): 711–716.

4. *Inside Higher Ed* reported in 2008 that 15 percent of students took the SAT three or more times. Both the SAT and the ACT incentivize repeat test-taking by allowing students to choose their best scores. Scott Jaschik, "The Evolving SAT Debates." *Inside Higher Ed*, June 23, 2008, www.insidehighered.com/news/2008/06/23/sat.

5. See Michaly Csikszentmihalyi, *Creativity: Flow and the Psychology of Discovery and Invention* (New York: HarperCollins, 1996), 108–109 for the mental space that optimizes creativity.

6. For resources on the power of storytelling, see Brian Boyd, *On the Origin of Stories: Evolution, Cognition, and Fiction* (Cambridge, MA: The Belknap Press of Harvard University Press, 2009); Lisa Cron, *Wired for Story* (Berkeley, CA: Ten Speed Press, 2012); Jonathan Gottschall, *The Storytelling Animal: How Stories Make Us Human* (New York: Houghton Mifflin Harcourt, 2012); and Peter Guber, *Tell to Win: Connect, Persuade, and Triumph with the Hidden Power of Story* (New York: Crown Business, 2011).

7. For background on Performance Theory, see Richard Schechner, *Performance Theory*. Rev. and expanded ed. (London: Routledge, 2003).

8. The New Common Application (CA4) can be accessed at www.commonapp.org.

9. See the Common Application for supplemental material.

10. The College Board recommends that students apply to five to eight schools and notes that most counselors don't recommend more than that. "How to Finalize Your College List," The College Board, last modified 2012, https://bigfuture.collegeboard.org/get-in/applying-101/how-to-finalize -your-college-list-admissions-college-application. In 2011, *U.S. News* reported the National Association for College Admission Counseling's findings that 25 percent or more students applied to seven or more schools in the fall of 2010. Katy Hopkins, "Study: More Students Apply

to More Colleges." *U.S. News,* October 20, 2011, www.usnews.com/education/best-colleges/articles/2011/10/20/study-more-students-apply-to-more-colleges.

11. For a summary of how and why the private admissions counseling business has grown over the past decade, see the following Independent Educational Consultants Association (IECA) reports: "Private College Counseling Profession Grows Despite Economy" (January, 2009) and "National Study Shows Dramatic Increase in Hiring Private College Counselors" (October 2009). Reports are available at www.iecaonline.com/news.html.

12. In 2010, the National Association for College Admission Counseling (NACAC) released a report entitled "Putting the College Admission 'Arms Race' in Context: An Analysis of Recent Trends in College Admissions and Their Effects on Institutional Policies and Practices." The report collects and analyzes data about the student and parent experience of the college process. It is available at www.nacacnet.org/research/PublicationsResources/Marketplace/discussion/Pages/CollegeAdmissionArmsRace.aspx.

13. Barbara A. Sorg and Paul Whitney, "The Effect of Trait Anxiety and Situational Stress on Working Memory Capacity," *Journal of Research in Personality* 26 (1992): 235–241.

14. The National Association for College Admission Counseling's (NACAC) 2012 State of College Admission Report identifies academic performance and strength of curriculum as the most important factors in the admissions decisions. To best succeed at the process, you should take the hardest courses you are able to and push yourself to go beyond the surface: get to know your teachers, your classmates, and the subject. SAT or ACT scores are the next most important thing. In a group of students who have similar grades and test scores, the essay is the differentiator. The NACAC's report is accessible at www.nacacnet.org/research/PublicationsResources/Marketplace/Documents/SOCA2011.pdf.

15. In his book *The Storytelling Animal*, Jonathan Gottschall discusses "mirror neurons," the neurons that fire in the brain that give us the impulse to mirror the actions represented in a story. The brain responds to the fictional stimuli the same way it responds to actual stimuli, and this explains our impulse to direct the heroine of a horror film to run for her life. Jonathan Gottschall, *The Storytelling Animal: How Stories Make Us Human* (New York: Houghton Mifflin Harcourt, 2012), 60–67. For a more in-depth analysis of brain functions, see Raymond A. Mar, "The Neuropsychology of Narrative: Story Comprehension, Story Production and Their Interrelation," *Neuropsychologia* 42 (2004): 1414–1434.

16. For a full account of how storytelling translates to effective leadership, see Peter Guber, *Tell to Win: Connect, Persuade, and Triumph with the Hidden Power of Story* (New York: Crown Business, 2011). See Gottschall and Mar. See also Lisa Cron, *Wired for Story* (Berkeley, CA: Ten Speed Press, 2012) and Daniel H. Pink, *A Whole New Mind: Why Right-Brainers Will Rule the Future* (New York: Riverhead Books, 2006), 100–129.

17. For examples of rules for a successful college essay, see Harry Bauld, *On Writing the College Application Essay: The Key to Acceptance at the College of Your Choice* (New York: Collins Reference, 2005) and Alan Gelb, *Conquering the College Admissions Essay in 10 Steps: Crafting a Winning Personal Statement* (Berkeley, CA: Ten Speed Press, 2008).

18. See Jean-Francois Rischard, *High Noon: 20 Global Problems, 20 Years to Solve Them* (New York: Basic Books, 2002), 69–87.

19. Tilmann Habermas and Susan Bluck, "Getting a Life: The Emergence of the Life Story in Adolescence," *The Psychological Bulletin* 126 (2000): 748–769.

20. Benjamin Elkin and Katherine Evans, *The Big Jump and Other Stories* (New York: Beginner Books, 1958).

A NOTE TO PARENTS

1. In 2012, the *New York Times* reported that 61 percent of students at the University of Florida changed majors within their first two years of study. Cecilia Capuzzi Simon, "Choosing One College Major Out of Hundreds," *New York Times*, November 2, 2012, www.nytimes.com/2012/11/04/education/edlife/choosing-one-college-major-out-of-hundreds.html.

CHAPTER 1: REFRESH

1. For a detailed discussion of the neuroscientific research, see Maria Konnikova, "The Power of Concentration." *New York Times*, December 15, 2012, www.nytimes.com/2012/12/16/opinion/sunday/the-power-of-concentration.html?pagewanted=all. See also Maria Konnikova, *Mastermind: How to Think Like Sherlock Holmes* (New York: Viking, 2003).

2. For a comprehensive guide to journaling and freeing your creativity, see Julia Cameron, *The Artist's Way* (New York: Penguin Group, 1992).

3. The Nun Study is an ongoing psychological study that began in 1986. It examines how cognitive function in a subject's early twenties, as measured by autobiographies, correlates to the onset of Alzheimer's later in life. The Nun Study has prompted many papers and much further research. The *New York Times* ran an article in 2001 that profiled several of the participants and summarized the findings. See Pam Belluck, "Nuns Offer Clues to Alzheimer's and Aging," *New York Times,* May 7, 2001, www.nytimes.com/2001/05/07/us/nuns-offer-clues-to-alzheimer-s-and-aging.html?pagewanted=all&src=pm.

4. For an overview of psychological evidence supporting this assertion, see Stanley M. Gully, Kara A. Incalcaterra, Aparma Joshi, and Matthew J. Beaubien, "A Meta-Analysis of Team-Efficacy, Potency, and Performance: Interdependence and Level of Analysis as Moderators of Observed Relationships," *Journal of Applied Psychology* 87 (2002): 819–832. The results of the study showed that there is a strong relationship between group work and efficacy.

5. Yale students who write daily themes win more writing contests than students from other schools. See Steve Engler, "Pen is mighty, for students of many majors," *The Yale Daily News,* April 21, 2004, http://yaledailynews.com/blog/2004/04/21/pen-is-mighty-for-students-of-many-majors.

6. For more on the habits of mind conducive to college readiness, see David T. Conley, *College Knowledge: What It Really Takes for Students to Succeed and What We Can Do to Get Them Ready* (San Francisco: Jossey-Bass, 2005).

7. For a full summary of brain functions, see Raymond A. Mar, "The Neuropsychology of Narrative: Story Comprehension, Story Production and Their Interrelation," *Neuropsychologia* 42 (2004): 1414–1434.

8. For a full examination of "flow"—what it means and how to achieve it—see Michaly Csikszentmihalyi, *Flow: The Psychology of Optimal Experience* (New York: Harper Perennial, 1991).

9. See Harry Bauld, *On Writing the College Application Essay: The Key to Acceptance at the College of Your Choice* (New York: Collins Reference, 2005) and Alan Gelb, *Conquering the College Admissions Essay in 10 Steps: Crafting a Winning Personal Statement* (Berkeley, CA: Ten Speed Press, 2008); Michele A. Hernandez, *Acing the College Application: How to Maximize Your Chances for Admission to the College of Your Choice* (New York: Ballatine Books, 2007); and Katherine Cohen, *How to Write a Killer College Application: Rock Hard Apps* (New York: Hyperion, 2003).

10. See Benjamin and Rosamund Stone Zander, *The Art of Possibility: Transforming Professional and Personal Life* (New York: Penguin Books, 2000), 45–53.

CHAPTER 2: BUILD A BRIDGE

1. P.L. Thomas, *Reading, Learning, Teaching Ralph Ellison* (New York: Peter Lang, 2008), 50.

2. See Jean-Francois Rischard, *High Noon: 20 Global Problems, 20 Years to Solve Them* (New York: Basic Books, 2002).

3. See Jim Collins, *Good to Great: Why Some Companies Make the Leap . . . and Others Don't* (New York: Harper Collins, 2001), 203.

4. Peter Cappelli, "Why Companies Aren't Getting the Employees They Need." *Wall Street Journal,* October 24, 2011, http://online.wsj.com/article/SB10001424052970204422404576596630897409182.html.

5. For tools to help you discover where you fit in the job market, see Tom Rath, *Strengths Finder 2.0.* (New York: Gallup Press, 2007) and Richard Nelson Bolles, *What Color Is Your Parachute?: A Practical Manual for Job-Hunters and Career-Changers*, 2013 ed., rev. ed. (Berkeley, CA: Ten Speed Press, 2013).

6. A great college tour virtual search engine is Campus Tours, last modified 2013, www.campustours.com/.

CHAPTER 3: TRANSFORM SCRIPTS TO STORIES

1. Hannah Arendt, *Men in Dark Times* (New York: Mariner Press, 1970), 105.
2. Daniel H. Pink, *A Whole New Mind: Why Right-Brainers Will Rule the Future* (New York: Riverhead Books, 2006), 100–115.
3. For an in-depth analysis of brain functions during storytelling, see Raymond A. Mar, "The Neuropsychology of Narrative: Story Comprehension, Story Production and Their Interrelation," *Neuropsychologia* 42 (2004): 1414–1434.
4. Emily Dickinson, "I'm Nobody!" in *The Poems of Emily Dickinson* (Cambridge, Mass: Harvard University Press, 1998), 206–207.
5. See Jonathan Gottschall, *The Storytelling Animal: How Stories Make Us Human* (New York: Houghton Mifflin Harcourt, 2012), 87–116. For a more in-depth analysis of brain functions, see Raymond A. Mar, "The Neuropsychology of Narrative: Story Comprehension, Story Production and Their Interrelation," *Neuropsychologia* 42 (2004): 1414–1434.
6. See Brian Boyd, *On the Origin of Stories: Evolution, Cognition, and Fiction* (Cambridge, MA: The Belknap Press of Harvard University Press), 139–140.

CHAPTER 4: CHOOSE A MOMENT

1. Abraham Verghese, *Cutting for Stone: A Novel* (New York: Vintage Books, 2009), 62.
2. See Gerald Huther, *The Compassionate Brain: How Empathy Creates Intelligence* (Boston: Trumpeter, 2006), 112–114.
3. For more on the habits of mind conducive to college readiness, see David T. Conley, *College Knowledge: What It Really Takes for Students to Succeed and What We Can Do to Get Them Ready* (San Francisco: Jossey-Bass, 2005).

CHAPTER 5: TELL IT OUT LOUD

1. Richard Langworth, *Churchill by Himself: The Definitive Collections of Quotations* (New York: Public Affairs, 2011).
2. For a full account of how storytelling translates to effective business leadership, see Peter Guber, *Tell to Win: Connect, Persuade, and Triumph with the Hidden Power of Story* (New York: Crown Business, 2011).
3. Every year, the National Association for Admissions Counseling (NACAC) releases a "State of College Admissions" report detailing current and trend data for college counseling and admissions. The 2011 report is available to the public at www.nacacnet.org/research/PublicationsResources/Marketplace/Documents/SOCA2011.pdf.
4. "Admission Staff Place Two Times More Importance on Authenticity in Student Essays than on Grammar and Punctuation, and More than Three Times More than Impressive Experiences," P.R. Newswire, last modified June 26, 2012, www.prnewswire.com/news-releases/admission-staff-place-two-times-more-importance-on-authenticity-in-student-essays-than-on-grammar-and-punctuation-and-more-than-three-times-more-than-on-impressive-experiences-160358895.html.

CHAPTER 6: WRITE IT OUT

1. Virginia Woolf. *Orlando: A Biography* (Ware: Wordsworth, 1995), 103.
2. For more information on Rosalind Franklin's life and research, see Anne Sayre, *Rosalind Franklin and DNA* (New York: W.W. Norton & Company, 1978).
3. In 2012, the *New York Times* reported that 61 percent of students at the University of Florida changed majors within their first two years of study. Cecilia Capuzzi Simon, "Choosing One College Major Out of Hundreds," *New York Times*, November 2, 2012, www.nytimes.com/2012/11/04/education/edlife/choosing-one-college-major-out-of-hundreds.html.

CHAPTER 7: FOCUS OUT

1. Larry Chang, ed., *Wisdom for the Soul: Five Millennia of Prescriptions for Spiritual Healing* (Washington, DC: Gnosophia Publishers, 2006), 473.

CHAPTER 8: MAP IT

1. Reif Larsen, *The Selected Works of T. S. Spivet* (New York: Penguin, 2009), 138.
2. For more on how the brain interprets narrative structure, see Lisa Cron, *Wired for Story* (Berkeley, CA: Ten Speed Press, 2012), 185–200.

CHAPTER 9: MAGNET AND GLOW

1. John Galsworthy, *The Forsyte Saga: Over the River* (London: Headline Book Publishing, 2009), 4.
2. Toni Morrison, *Beloved* (New York: Everyman's Library, 2006), 9.
3. Joseph Conrad, *Lord Jim* (New York: Empire Books, 2012), 1.
4. Tracy Kidder, *Mountains Beyond Mountains* (New York: Random House Trade Paperbacks, 2009), 3.
5. Eric Ries, *The Lean Startup* (New York: Crown Business, 2011), 149–184.

CHAPTER 10: EXPLORE PERSPECTIVES

1. Johann Wolfgang Goethe, *Wisdom and Experience*, trans. Hermann J. Weigand (London: Routledge & Kegan Paul LTD, 1949), 165.
2. The Viewpoints theatrical method explores characterization through improvisation, movement, and gesture. For a full view of the technique, see Anne Bogart and Tina Landau, *The Viewpoints Books: A Practical Guide to Viewpoints and Composition* (New York: Theatre Communications Group, 2005).

CHAPTER 11: RAISE THE STAKES

1. Jo Ann Boydston, Patricia Baysinger, Barbara Levine, and Sidney Hook. *The Middle Works of John Dewey 1899–1924* (Carbondale, Ill.: Southern Illinois University Press, 2008), 361.
2. "Gabby Giffords Statement at Gun Violence Hearing," January 30, 2013. Video Clip. YouTube. www.youtube.com/watch?v=thOhDNfyvRc.
3. Peter Guber, *Tell to Win: Connect, Persuade, and Triumph with the Hidden Power of Story* (New York: Crown Business, 2011), 217–246.
4. Daniel H. Pink, *A Whole New Mind: Why Right-Brainers Will Rule the Future* (New York: Riverhead Books, 2006), 100–115.

CHAPTER 12: WRITE OUT LOUD

1. Quote used with permission from Elyn Saks.
2. Charna Halpern, Del Close, and Kim Johnson. *Truth in Comedy: The Manual of Improvisation* (Colorado Springs, Colorado: Meriwether Publishing, 1994), 79.
3. See Paul Tough, *How Children Succeed: Grit, Curiosity, and the Hidden Power of Character* (New York: Houghton Mifflin Harcourt, 2012).
4. See Karen Reivich and Andrew Shatte, *The Resilience Factor: 7 Keys to Finding Your Inner Strength and Overcoming Life's Hurdles* (New York: Broadway Books, 2003), 9–30.